PERRY'S

DEPARTMENT STORE

A Buying Simulation

4TH EDITION

PERRY'S
DEPARTMENT STORE

A Buying Simulation
4TH EDITION

Karen M. Videtic

Cynthia W. Steele

Fairchild Books An Imprint of Bloomsbury Publishing Inc.

BLOOMSBURY
LONDON · NEW DELHI · NEW YORK · SYDNEY

FAIRCHILD BOOKS

An imprint of Bloomsbury Publishing Inc

1385 Broadway   50 Bedford Square
New York   London
NY 10018   WC1B 3DP
USA   UK

www.bloomsbury.com

FAIRCHILD BOOKS, BLOOMSBURY and the Diana logo
are trademarks of Bloomsbury Publishing Plc

Second edition published 2003

Third edition published 2009

This edition first published 2015

© Bloomsbury Publishing Inc, 2015

Library of Congress Cataloging-in-Publication Data 2014025050
A catalog record for this book is available from the Library of Congress

ISBN: 9781628920154

Typeset by Lachina
Cover Design by Untitled
Printed and bound in the United States of America

Contents

Preface   xi

About the Authors   xv

Acknowledgments   xvii

Introduction: Perry's Background Information   1

CHAPTER 1   Step 1: Redefine Your Customer   17

CHAPTER 2   Step 2: Research Current Market and Fashion Trends   25

CHAPTER 3   Step 3: Develop Buying Plan   31

CHAPTER 4   Step 4: Develop Assortment Plan   53

CHAPTER 5   Step 5: How to Shop the Market   67

CHAPTER 6   Step 6: Plan Market Purchases   77

CHAPTER 7   Step 7: Negotiate Profitability   89

CHAPTER 8   Step 8: Examine the Income Statement   101

CHAPTER 9   The Buyer's Role in Product Development   107

CHAPTER 10 Career Opportunities in Retail Buying   117

APPENDIX A Website Resources   125

APPENDIX B Retailing Formulas   127

Glossary   130

Bibliography   135

Index   137

Extended Contents

	Preface	xi
	About the Authors	xv
	Acknowledgments	xvii
	Introduction: Perry's Background Information	1
	Objectives of the Simulation	1
	The Simulation: What Is It and How Does It Work?	2
	Perry's Retail Organizational Structure	2
	The Role and Responsibilities of a Perry's Buyer	3
	Perry's Demographic Information	5
	Perry's Statistical Information	9
	The Simulation Begins	15
CHAPTER 1	Step 1: Redefine Your Customer	17
	VALS	17
	Cultural Differences	22
CHAPTER 2	Step 2: Research Current Market and Fashion Trends	25
	The Fashion Office	27
	The Buying and Merchandise Flow Calendar	28
CHAPTER 3	Step 3: Develop Buying Plan	31
	Planning Sales	36
	Planning Beginning-of-the-Month Stock (BOM Stock)	41
	Turnover	42
	Planning Markdowns	46
	Planning Purchases	49
	Open-To-Buy	51
CHAPTER 4	Step 4: Develop Assortment Plan	53
	Classifications	53
	Monthly Sales by Classification	54

	Subclassifications	56
	Other Factors in Assortment Planning	59
	Price Lines	59
CHAPTER 5	Step 5: How to Shop the Market	67
	Pre-Market Planning	68
	Research Business Statistics	69
	Planning Your Market Itinerary	70
	Getting Organized	71
	Discovering Trends While in the Market	71
	Market Assessment and Decision Making	72
	Developing Key Resources	73
	The Buyer's Role in Market	74
	Shopping International Markets	74
CHAPTER 6	Step 6: Plan Market Purchases	77
	Preplanning	77
	Open-to-Buy	81
	Visiting Resources	81
	Writing Purchase Orders	83
	Delivery Dates	86
	Terms of the Sale	86
	Transportation	87
	Buying Calendar and Merchandise Flow	88
CHAPTER 7	Step 7: Negotiate Profitability	89
	Negotiation Preparation	89
	Relationship Power	90
	Negotiation Meeting	91
	Closing the Negotiations	92
	Negotiation of Purchases	93
	Negotiation of Payment Terms	93
	Negotiation of Freight Charges	94
	Negotiation of Price and Discounts	94
	Negotiation of Allowances	95
	Cancellations	98

Cross-Cultural Negotiation   99

Relevance of Time in Cross-Cultural Negotiation   99

Personal Space   100

CHAPTER 8   Step 8: Examine the Income Statement   101

Profit or Loss?   101

Components of the Income Statement   102

Sales   102

Cost of Goods Sold   102

Gross Margin   104

Operating Expenses   104

Net Other Income   105

CHAPTER 9   The Buyer's Role in Product Development   107

Background   107

Branding   108

Product Planning   108

Salability   109

Fabric   109

Specification and Costing Sheets   109

Sourcing   114

Testing   114

Labeling   114

Shipping   115

Technology   115

Summary   116

CHAPTER 10   Career Opportunities in Retail Buying   117

Overview   117

Careers   118

Merchandise Assistant, Merchandise Coordinator   118

Business Analyst, Merchandise Analyst, or Merchandise Allocator   118

Planner   119

Manager of Planning and Distribution   119

Director of Distribution and Planning   120

Assistant Buyer   120

Associate Buyer, Senior Assistant Buyer   **121**

Buyer, Senior Buyer   **121**

Divisional Merchandise Manager   **121**

General Merchandise Manager   **122**

Buying Groups and Services   **122**

The Internet   **122**

APPENDIX A   Website Resources   **125**
APPENDIX B   Retailing Formulas   **127**

Glossary   **130**
Bibliography   **135**
Index   **137**

Preface

Perry's Department Store: A Buying Simulation, 4th Edition, launches students into the exciting role of being a retail buyer in the fashion industry using a unique simulation approach that takes readers step-by-step through a real-life buying experience. The text is organized into 10 chapters that walk students through the various steps a new buyer would take to complete a six-month buying plan and a merchandise assortment plan for the women's contemporary apparel, junior apparel, women's accessories, men's apparel and accessories, men's contemporary apparel, children's, or home furnishings markets. It has been the authors' experience that students have difficulty with the application of mathematical models even though they are competent in the initial use of these formulas. This reorganized and updated text strengthens students' understanding of buyers' responsibilities by bridging the gap between the principles of retail buying and mathematical formulas and concepts.

This edition of *Perry's Department Store* takes on a new dimension with a more realistic perspective of today's global fashion marketplace by expanding Perry's to a 39-branch upscale department store located between the Washington, DC metropolitan area extending south to the affluent region of south Florida. Updated demographic information is provided, and articles about diversity and affluent buying behaviors are included in the text and website. Students should become familiar with merchandising mathematics before they begin this simulation. There are numerous textbooks that cover this material, and will be helpful as you work through the Perry's Department Store simulation.

NEW TO THIS EDITION

* A companion website, *Perry's Department Store A Buying Simulation STUDIO, 4th Edition* now allows the student to follow the text's sequences and perform the corresponding steps, access information from the web, download spreadsheets and worksheets, and complete calculations more comfortably.

* Numbered worksheets on the website correspond with the textbook.

* New industry statistics and trend reports have been added for women's contemporary apparel, junior apparel, women's accessories, men's apparel and accessories, men's contemporary apparel, children's and home furnishings departments.

* Updated information is included on additional departments and different markets, classifications and resources, information on customer profiles, census data, and statistics.

* Critical analysis of the luxury marketplace is explored through psychographics and demographics.

STUDIO

Fairchild Books has a long history of excellence in textbook publishing for fashion education. Our new online STUDIOs are specially developed to complement this book with rich media ancillaries that students can adapt to their visual learning styles. *Perry's Department Store A Buying Simulation STUDIO, 4th edition* features online self-quizzes with results and personalized study tips. It allows students to follow the text's steps and calculations with data and statistical information, worksheets, Excel® spreadsheets with embedded formulas and blank worksheets, industry catalogs and private label line sheets, and web links to additional resources to complete the buying simulation. The website contains more visual demographic and psychographic information about the Perry's consumer, apparel, and home fashion operating statistics, plus material for buyers from manufacturers and a trend analyst.

STUDIO access cards are offered free with new book purchases and also sold separately through Bloomsbury Fashion Central (www.BloomsburyFashionCentral .com).

Key Features:

* Industry statistics and trend reports are included for women's contemporary apparel, junior apparel, women's accessories, men's apparel and accessories, men's contemporary apparel, children's, and home furnishings, with new categories added for the women's accessories, women's contemporary, and men's contemporary markets.

* Industry catalogs and private label line lists, which are not typically accessible to students, are also included.

* Downloadable Excel spreadsheets are now available with and without the formulas embedded, and links to additional sources allow students to apply what they learn in different contexts.

* Links are provided to GeoVALS profiles and pie charts with additional consumer research profiles.

* Links are provided to census data and statistics, giving students access to the most up-to-date information.

ORGANIZATION OF THE TEXT

Perry's Department Store: A Buying Simulation is organized into an introductory chapter plus 10 chapters that correspond with the steps of the buying simulation. The book begins with background information about the fictitious Perry's Department Store, so students can become familiar with their new department and industry. As would any competent buyer, students must research new market and industry trends. Links in both the text and Perry's Department Store: A Buying Simulation STUDIO assist students in accessing contemporary information and research materials that will improve their merchandising decisions. When they become knowledgeable about their area, students proceed by projecting sales, beginning-of-the-month stock requirements, and markdowns to complete the six-month plan.

It is not enough to project capital investment in merchandise. A buyer must be able to spend the dollar plan in the most effective and profitable way possible. The next step the new Perry's buyer—the student—takes is to develop a merchandise assortment plan. This begins with the development of merchandise classifications and subclassifications, and culminates with an assortment plan detailing units purchased by price line, dollar, size, fabrication, and color.

No buyer's job would be complete without planning market trips and writing orders for actual merchandise. This edition explores how to effectively and efficiently shop the market in a global marketplace and discusses negotiation skills. Although not all of the buyer's open-to-buy is spent, the simulation is almost complete when line lists from actual manufacturers are used to purchase appropriate merchandise for the department.

Today's department store buyer must find a niche to remain competitive with the numerous upscale department stores and specialty retailers. Sales promotion has become one tool to help buyers compete in the marketplace. Therefore, this simulation discusses the use of advertising, publicity, and public relations as they relate to an individual buyer's perspective, and examines their ability to increase the sales of a department.

Although few buyers look beyond the gross margin of an income statement, the authors feel that students need to see the total financial picture to understand the buyer's role in making a department profitable. The book therefore includes a chapter on profit and income statements as they relate to Perry's Department Store.

Product development has emerged as a vital method for buyers and their departments to remain competitive. Steps in the creation of a private label of merchandise for the target customer are discussed, along with the importance of fabric, sourcing, delivery, and technology.

Positions in retail buying—from assistant to general merchandise manager—are described in the final chapter. Included, too, are opportunities within buying groups.

The most significant feature of this text and Perry's Department Store: A Buying Simulation STUDIO is the ability to replicate real-life experience for students, so they can better understand the retail buyer's role. The nature of simulation requires that students create an up-to-date business environment as they research current market and industry trends. The combination of the text and the website demands that students continually provide the most current and contemporary information necessary to make their buying decisions. This keeps the text relevant over time and ensures that students understand how to remain current in their field through research.

Actual line lists of manufacturers offer a realistic sampling of the real world as it relates to buying. The charts and forms in this book and website are replicas of those found in the retail and wholesale industry. They expose students to the procedures and policies they can expect to find in a first job as an assistant buyer or as a buying office clerk. Students may copy blank forms from the book or manipulate them electronically on the website to use for worksheets and practice.

INSTRUCTOR'S RESOURCES

An instructor's guide is available and includes a sample course outline and syllabi, grading rubrics, additional real-world student examples, links to fashion websites, demographic and census websites, and articles for classroom discussion. Worksheets are provided with and without embedded formulas, and completed worksheets can act as a guideline for faculty evaluation. This guide also helps the instructor who has never been a buyer and who may need additional information about resources, terminology, and other aspects unique to retail buying.

About the Authors

KAREN M. VIDETIC, former chairperson and professor in the Department of Fashion Design and Merchandising at Virginia Commonwealth University (VCU) in Richmond, Virginia, has taught retail buying, fashion branding, and fashion merchandising in VCU's Department of Fashion Design and Merchandising since 1984. Her bachelor's degree in marketing and distributive education, her Master's of Education in human resource development, and considerable coursework toward a doctorate in urban services were all earned at VCU.

In 1997, Professor Videtic spent five months at the University of Ballarat outside of Melbourne, Australia, as a lecturer for the School of Business. She taught buyer behavior, contemporary issues in management, and human resource development on a graduate level. She has also taught in Florence, Italy, in a summer co-curricular study abroad program that integrated fashion design and merchandising with graphic and interior design students in an international branding project. Professor Videtic's retail experience extends from department stores to local boutiques, in both management, fashion promotion, and fashion buying. On the wholesale side of the fashion industry, Professor Videtic has assisted several independent manufacturers' sales representatives in both intimate apparel and fine jewelry, and attended New York, Las Vegas, and Atlanta markets. Professor Videtic continues her consulting work, which includes merchandise planning for independent retailers, forecasting, rebranding, and management seminars for numerous professional organizations.

CYNTHIA W. STEELE is vice president of product development for Split P, a wholesale company specializing in tabletop and home décor textiles and furnishings. She is responsible for the design direction for the brand and travels internationally to source product.

Previously, she was creative manager for C & F Enterprises, Inc., and Gallerie II, a wholesale company offering bedding, home décor, and seasonal gifts. Before joining C & F, she was vice president of product development for Evergreen Enterprises, Inc., a wholesale operation of flags, garden, and home décor products. Preceding Evergreen, Ms. Steele was a national account executive for New Creative Enterprises and Square Nest, a wholesaler of giftware and decorative accessories for the home and garden.

She has also served as director of national accounts for Silvestri, a manufacturer of giftware, decorative accessories and seasonal collections. Prior to joining Silvestri, Ms. Steele was operations manager for a manufacturer's representative firm.

Formerly an assistant professor in the Department of Fashion at VCU, she has taught courses in apparel industry, retail buying, merchandising, trends, and fashion promotion. Her professional background includes more than 15 years' experience in retail buying and management for department, specialty, and independent stores. She has worked in children's wear, misses', juniors', and women's sportswear, bridal and formalwear, men's wear, and fashion jewelry and accessories.

Ms. Steele earned a bachelor of fine arts in fashion design and a master's of education in adult education. Both degrees are from VCU.

Acknowledgments

DEIDRA ARRINGTON, Assistant Professor, Virginia Commonwealth University

JASON BECKWITH, Sales Manager East Coast, Daniel Rainne

PATRICIA BREMAN, Senior Consultant, Strategic Business Insights

CAROLINE DODSON, Accessories Designer

MICHAEL FISHER, Creative Director/Trend Forecasting Men's Wear/Lifestyle/Culture, Fashion Snoops

NANCY GIANNI, President and CEO, Rock Me!

JAYHAYRA HARRELL, Marketing and Public Relations, Prps

ANNA MUZZY, Vice President and COO, Rock Me!

BETTINA PEACEMAKER, Assistant Head for Academic Outreach and Business Research Librarian, Virginia Commonwealth University

ROSHELLA RICKER, Senior Buyer Women's Wovens, Urban Outfitters

JOMARIE SANFILIPPO, Buyer, Saks Fifth Avenue

JILL STEIN, Sales Major Accounts and Boutiques, BB Dakota

MARTY METZLER, President/CEO, Park Designs and Split P

STEVEN BORSCH, President/CEO, Marketing Directions, Inc.

Perry's Background Information

* What a simulation is and how it is used
* The statistical and demographic information needed to make buying decisions
* How to analyze statistical information to define a customer base
* The breadth of a buyer's job and the function of the buyer within the retail organization

This chapter explains the simulation aspect of this textbook. It introduces a fictitious flagship store and its 38 branch locations throughout the southeastern United States, and the pending first international branch store in Dubai, United Arab Emirates. The location, sales volume, merchandise assortment, and customer profile are different for each branch. Buying assortments are organized by classifying or grouping stores according to their performance, target customer, and geographic location. Assuming the role of a newly promoted buyer, the student must research demographics and statistics, learn about market segmentation, and confront the responsibilities of a retail buyer. A step-by-step plan must be initiated before a market trip for the fall/holiday season.

OBJECTIVES OF THE SIMULATION

After completing the simulation in this book, students will be able to:

* Understand how and why buying decisions are made, as demonstrated through this buying simulation

* Understand the breadth of the buyer's role in a retail organization

* Research market trends and industry trends

* Apply buying formulas and mathematical examples in a realistic format

* Plan model stock for a department within a retail organization

* Understand how market segmentation is used in a retail setting, in particular, the luxury marketplace

* Understand the role of the buyer in the product development process

* Recognize the changing responsibilities of the buyer today

THE SIMULATION: WHAT IS IT AND HOW DOES IT WORK?

A simulation can be defined as a similar situation, resembling, but not exactly like, the conditions that exist in reality. For the sake of this simulation, you will be provided with the statistical and demographic information necessary to make buying decisions. It will be your responsibility to supply the logic and the supplemental materials to substantiate your merchandising decisions.

PERRY'S RETAIL ORGANIZATIONAL STRUCTURE

The merchandising function at Perry's Department Store involves the purchasing of merchandise for retail sale. The vice president of merchandising oversees *general merchandise managers (GMMs)*, *divisional merchandise managers (DMMs)*, retail planners and allocators, buyers, and assistant buyers. The vice president of operations is responsible for handling all aspects of the retail stores. Reporting to the vice president of operations are the warehouse and store managers, department sales managers, and salespeople. The fashion office, lead by the fashion director, is a staff or advisory position that reports to both the general merchandise manager and the vice president of sales promotion about fashion trends that impact both merchandise and fashion presentation. The vice president of sales promotion is in charge of advertising, public relations, social media, and visual merchandising. Accounts payable/receivable, inventory control, customer charge accounts, merchandise information systems, and finance are controlled by the vice president of finance. The vice president of human resources is responsible for the hiring, maintaining, and training of store personnel. Buyers at Perry's, as with any department store, must interact with all functions to maximize the potential and profit of their department.

As you will see in Figure I.1, Perry's is organized as a traditional department store, with five functions and a fashion office reporting to the general merchandise manager and the vice president of sales promotion.

THE ROLE AND RESPONSIBILITIES OF A PERRY'S BUYER

Buying and selling functions are separated at Perry's. This means that buyers do not directly supervise the sales staff. However, because of the nature of luxury products, buyers are significantly involved with sales training and merchandise layout for the departmental sales floor.

The responsibilities of a buyer employed by Perry's include:

1. Development of a six-month dollar buying plan for all stores in conjunction with the planner

2. Development of model stock plans by classification, subclassification, price line, color, units, size, and fabrication for all stores

3. Trend analysis (in report form)
   a. Use of fashion office as a main source of trend information

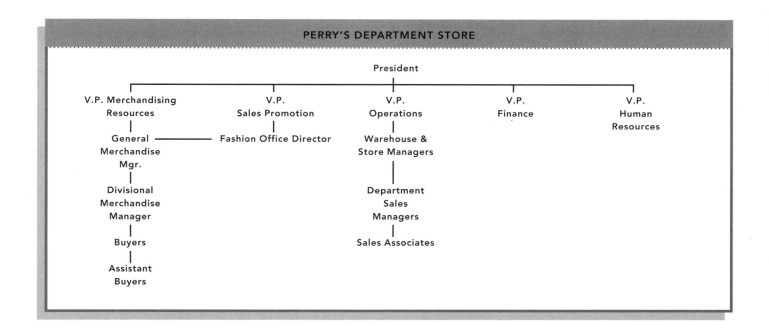

FIGURE I.1 Organization chart for Perry's Department Store

4. Vendor analysis (in report form)
   a. Sales performance
   b. Markdown allowance (dollars and percentages)

5. Education of sales personnel, to include:
   a. Merchandising of new trends
   b. Front- and forward-featured merchandise schedule
   c. Sales promotions and special events

6. Supervision of assistant buyers and other buying office staff

7. Development of long-range departmental goals including the ranking and clustering of retail branches

8. Selection of merchandise at market according to approved plans

9. Accurate recording of all purchases, transfers, and returns to vendors that affect the value of departmental inventory

10. Promotional plans for department, to include:
    a. Merchandise signage
    b. Cooperative advertising assistance (vendor and dollars)
    c. Merchandise to be promoted
    d. Social media

11. Communication with department's sales managers, to include:
    a. Sales goals (daily/monthly)
    b. Shortage goals
    c. Special promotions (advertising, fashion shows, etc.)
    d. Markdowns and transfer requests

12. Communication with divisional merchandise manager and general merchandise managers, to include:
    a. Accurate and timely stock plans
    b. Presentation of orders for approval
    c. Sales data
    d. Updates on open-to-buy

Perry's Department Store is fictitious, as is the statistical information, and is in no way representative of a specific retail organization.

Perry's is an upscale, specialty department store headquartered in Fredericksburg, Virginia. The flagship store is located in downtown Fredericksburg, with 38 branch operations in premium shopping malls and neighborhoods in major metropolitan areas throughout the southeastern United States. Cities include Washington, DC and surrounding communities in Virginia and Maryland; Richmond, Williamsburg, and Virginia Beach, Virginia; Raleigh and Charlotte, North Carolina; Savannah and Atlanta, Georgia, and surrounding areas; Charleston, Hilton Head, and Columbia, South Carolina; and Jacksonville, Orlando, Tampa, West Palm Beach, Miami Beach, and southwestern Florida.

Fredericksburg is located approximately 45 miles south of Washington, DC, and 45 miles north of Richmond, Virginia. It is a suburb of the Washington area, and a commuter train currently connects Union Station in Washington with downtown Fredericksburg. The headquarters of Perry's is in perfect proximity to the New York City apparel industry and offers easy access to fashion market weeks and relatively inexpensive trips to market for immediate purchases. The New York City market, which can be reached by a four-hour train ride or a 40-minute flight, offers the right merchandise for Perry's upscale, affluent customer.

Perry's Department Store was founded in 1918 by Mr. Robert Perry in downtown Washington, DC, where he provided apparel to wealthy politicians, government officials, diplomats, and their wives and families. As the store's reputation grew, so did the number of stores, expanding into the surrounding areas of Virginia and Maryland.

In 1958, Perry's headquarters was moved to Fredericksburg as the expansion of cities and suburban flight influenced the growth of cities up and down the East Coast. Eventually, Robert Perry's sons, Brandon and Thomas, took over the reins of the store and slowly expanded the very successful operation throughout the major cities in the Southeast. Led by CEO Justin Lindsay, Perry's Department Store went public in 1993 and trades on the New York Stock Exchange.

Today, Perry's generates around $894 million in annual sales and $78 million in profits. This equates to about $525 in sales per square foot. Perry's key competitors are Saks Fifth Avenue, Neiman Marcus, Nordstrom, and Bloomingdale's, and its operating performance is comparable to these retail operations with a similar customer base.

Tables I.1 and I.2 include some demographic statistics for the northern Virginia, Maryland, West Virginia, and District of Columbia metropolitan locations of Perry's Department Store. The U.S. Census American Factfinder was used to collect this data and can be used to research additional data about this metropolitan area or any other metropolitan areas.

Go to: http://factfinder2.census.gov/faces/nav/jsf/pages/index.xhtml

TABLE 1.1

WASHINGTON–ARLINGTON–ALEXANDRIA, DC–VA–MD–WV METROPOLITAN STATISTICAL AREA U.S. CENSUS BUREAU

The area includes the following counties, districts, and independent cities.

DISTRICT OF COLUMBIA

* Washington, D.C.

MARYLAND: THE FOLLOWING COUNTIES ARE CATEGORIZED AS PART OF THE WASHINGTON–ARLINGTON–ALEXANDRIA, DC–VA–MD–WV METROPOLITAN STATISTICAL AREA:

* Calvert County
* Charles County
* Frederick County
* Montgomery County
* Prince George's County

VIRGINIA: COUNTIES AND INDEPENDENT CITIES (INDEPENDENT CITIES ARE LISTED UNDER THEIR SURROUNDING COUNTY OR PARENT COUNTY):

* Arlington County
  * City of Alexandria
* Clarke County
* Culpeper County
* Fairfax County
  * City of Fairfax
  * City of Falls Church
* Fauquier County
* Loudoun County
* Prince William County
  * City of Manassas
  * City of Manassas Park

continued

TABLE I.I (CONTINUED)

WASHINGTON–ARLINGTON–ALEXANDRIA, DC–VA–MD–WV
METROPOLITAN STATISTICAL AREA
U.S. CENSUS BUREAU

VIRGINIA: COUNTIES AND INDEPENDENT CITIES (INDEPENDENT CITIES ARE LISTED UNDER THEIR SURROUNDING COUNTY OR PARENT COUNTY):

* Rappahannock County
* Spotsylvania County
  * City of Fredericksburg
* Stafford County
* Warren County

WEST VIRGINIA

* Jefferson County

ALTHOUGH ASSOCIATED WITH THE WASHINGTON METROPOLITAN AREA, THE FOLLOWING COUNTIES ARE CATEGORIZED AS PART OF THE BALTIMORE–TOWSON, MD METROPOLITAN STATISTICAL AREA:

* Anne Arundel County
* Howard County

ALTHOUGH ASSOCIATED WITH THE WASHINGTON METROPOLITAN AREA, THE FOLLOWING COUNTY IS CATEGORIZED AS PART OF THE CALIFORNIA-LEXINGTON PARK, MD METROPOLITAN AREA:

* St. Mary's County

Table I.2

				MEDIAN	EDUCATION:	% HOUSEHOLD	
METROPOLITAN AREA	POPULATION	MEDIAN AGE	EMPLOYED IN MANAGEMENT	HOUSEHOLD INCOME	HS OR HIGHER	INCOME OVER $100,000	MEAN FAMILY INCOME
WASHINGTON DC METROPOLITAN DEMOGRAPHICS							
Washington, DC	601,723	33.8	40.0%	$ 61,835.00	87.1%	41.0%	$ 96,183.00
VIRGINIA							
Arlington, VA	207,627	33.4	67.2%	$ 99,651.00	92.6%	48.9%	$ 128,300.00
Fairfax County, VA	1,081,726	37.3	56.2%	108,439	91.9%	54.7%	$ 154,187.00
Clarke County, VA	14,034	44.9	43.1%	$ 80,186.00	89.3%	45.2%	$ 111,740.00
Culpepper County, VA	46,689	38.8	35.4%	$ 65,567.00	83.5%	33.7%	$ 85,477.00
Fairfax County, VA	1,081,726	37.3	55.8%	$ 109,383.00	91.6%	55.0%	$ 157,253.00
Fauquier County, VA	65,203	41.3	42.5%	$ 88,687.00	91.0%	43.6%	$ 124,774.00
Loudon County, VA	312,511	34.8	56.1%	$ 122,068.00	93.4%	61.3%	$ 151,282.00
Prince William County, VA	402,002	33.5	43.6%	$ 96,160.00	88.9%	47.7%	$ 120,831.00
Rappahannock County, VA	7,373	47.5	25.7%	$ 35,067.00	82.1%	6.3%	$ 53,782.00
Spotsylvannia County, VA	122,397	35.3	39.3%	$ 79,402.00	88.9%	36.8%	$ 99,811.00
Stafford County, VA	128,961	34.6	44.8%	$ 96,355.00	92.1%	47.6%	$ 117,267.00
Warren County, VA	37,575	39.7	29.8%	$ 61,693.00	84.8%	24.2%	$ 86,896.00
CITIES IN VIRGINIA:							
Alexandria, VA	139,996	35.6	58.3%	$ 82,899.00	91.0%	41.1%	$ 142,422.00
Fairfax City, VA	22,565	39.1	53%	$ 98,563.00	92.5%	49.5%	$ 134,178.00
McLean, VA	48,000	45.1	75.9%	$ 170,933.00	98.0%	78.8%	$ 238,841.00
Falls Church, VA	12,332	39	68%	$ 122,844.00	96.3%	58.8%	$ 173,758.00
Manassas, VA	37,821	32.1	33%	$ 70,634.00	82.2%	32.6%	$ 92,901.00
Manassas Park, Va	14,273	30.9	30.2%	$ 71,810.00	79.8%	29.2%	$ 90,260.00
Fredericksburg, VA	24,286	28.8	40.5%	$ 45,951.00	89.1%	19.4%	$ 83,647.00

continued

TABLE I.2 (CONTINUED)

WASHINGTON DC METROPOLITAN DEMOGRAPHICS							
METROPOLITAN AREA	POPULATION	MEDIAN AGE	EMPLOYED IN MANAGEMENT	MEDIAN HOUSEHOLD INCOME	EDUCATION: HS OR HIGHER	% HOUSEHOLD INCOME OVER $100,000	MEAN FAMILY INCOME
MARYLAND							
Calvert County, MD	88,737	40.1	40.1%	$ 92,395.00	92.3%	46.3%	$ 117,641.00
Charles County, MD	146,551	37.4	41.8%	$ 93,063.00	92%	46%	$ 114,912.00
Frederick County, MD	2,333,385	38.6	45.8%	$ 83,706.00	91.8%	41.0%	$ 110,650.00
Montongomery County, MD	971,777	38.5	56.0%	$ 96,985.000	91.0%	48.7%	$ 152,279.00
Prince George's County, MD	863,420	34.9	38%	$ 73,568.00	85.6%	33.8%	$ 99,470.00
CITIES IN MARYLAND							
Bethesda, MD	60,858	42.5	75.3%	$ 141,817.00	98.2%	65.2%	$ 260,826.00
Chevy Chase, MD	9,545	45.6	76.8%	$ 157,802.00	96.6%	68.0%	$ 288,835.00
WEST VIRGINIA							
Jefferson County, WV	53,498	38.9	39.7%	$ 64,314.00	86.2%	27.1%	$ 88,833.00

SOURCE: U.S. Census American Factfinder

PERRY'S STATISTICAL INFORMATION

Perry's classifies its branch stores by a ranking of A, B, or C, according to sales volume, trading area demographics and psychographics, and the progressive styling of the consumer who patronizes each branch. Many department stores rank their branch stores this way, using an alphabetical ranking system; others may use similar methods. Some of the reasons why stores are ranked in this manner are to plan the following:

* Sales volume

* Square footage

* Consumer profile

* Interior décor

* Fixtures

* Inventory levels

* Stock assortment

* Store personnel

A stores have the highest sales volume and usually receive an additional layer of upscale, fashion merchandise. Typically, A stores have a higher average purchase than B or C stores. B stores have the next highest sales volume and inventory levels. C stores produce less sales volume than A and B stores and have an inventory that reflects the taste level of a more conservative consumer who spends less and is attracted to more moderate brands.

At Perry's, A stores generate a sales volume close to or above $30.7 million and cater to an ultra-affluent consumer with fashion-forward progressive taste and a significant discretionary income. These consumers are managerial professionals or entrepreneurs who tend to work in an office environment. They want to be the first in their community to wear a new style or designer, and they are considered fashion leaders in their peer group. Quality and service are very important to them.

Perry's B stores produce an average sales volume of $17.9 million, obtained from upper-middle-income individuals who value quality, designer/brand-name merchandise, and the social reference point that comes with wearing a certain article of clothing or accessory. Although they have less discretionary income, they are socially driven to purchase the "right fashion at the right time."

Perry's has eight C stores that produce a lower sales volume of approximately $16.8 million per store. These stores are patronized by consumers who place importance on fashion brands but are less concerned with the best quality. However, they are very concerned with the right look but at the right price. They are influenced by their social network and their work environment. C store consumers are practical and rationalize their purchases with their lifestyle.

Table I.3 shows how Perry's rates its stores according to the sales volume, competition, location, and the progressive styling of the consumer who patronizes each branch. Table I.4 details the average store sales by rank and the percentage of stores within each ranking.

TABLE I.3

			PERRY'S STORE LOCATIONS, RANKINGS CLUSTERS		
NAME	**LOCATION**	**METRO AREA**	**ANCHORS**	**STORE RANK**	**CLUSTER**
FLORIDA (13)					
Aventura Mall	Aventura, FL	Miami	Nordstrom, Bloomingdale's, Macy's	B	3/Florida
Boca Raton Town Center	Boca Raton, FL	Miami	Nordstrom, Bloomingdale's, Macy's	B	3/Florida
Worth Avenue	Palm Beach, FL	Miami	Saks 5th Avenue, Neiman Marcus	A	3/Florida
Galleria Fort Lauderdale	Fort Lauderdale, FL	Central East Coast	Saks 5th Avenue, Nordstrom	A	3/Florida
Bal Harbour	Miami, FL	Miami	Saks 5th Avenue, Neiman Marcus	A	3/Florida
The Mall at Wellington Green	Wellington, FL	Central East Coast	Nordstrom, Dillards, Macy's	C	3/Florida
International Plaza	Tampa, FL	Tampa/Clearwater	Saks 5th Avenue, Nordstrom, Neiman Marcus	A	3/Florida
Bell Tower Shops	Fort Myers, FL	Southwest Florida	Saks 5th Avenue, Tommy Bahama	B	3/Florida
Waterside Shops	Naples, FL	Southwest Florida	Saks 5th Avenue, Nordstrom	A	3/Florida
The Mall at Millenia	Orlando, FL	Central Florida	Neiman Marcus, Bloomingdales	A	3/Florida
Florida Mall	Orlando, FL	Central Florida	Saks 5th Avenue, Nordstrom, Macy's	B	3/Florida
The Falls	Meance, FL	Miami Metro	Bloomingdales, Macy's	C	3/Florida
The Gardens Mall	Palm Beach, FL	Miami Metro	Nordstrom, Bloomingdales	B	3/Florida
GEORGIA (5)					
Savannah, GA Downtown	Savannah, GA	Southeast coast	Boutiques, Belk	B	2/Central
Lenox Mall	Atlanta, GA	Atlanta Metro	Bloomingdales, Neiman Marcus	A	2/Central
Phipps Plaza	Atlanta, GA	Atlanta Metro	Saks 5th Avenue, Nordstrom	A	2/Central
Perimeter Mall	Atlanta, GA	Atlanta Metro	Norsdstrom, Dillards, Macy's	B	2/Central
The Mall of Georgia	Buford, GA	Atlanta Metro	Nordstrom, Belk, Dillards	C	2/Central
NORTH CAROLINA (4)					
South Park Mall	Charlotte, NC	Charlotte metro	Neiman Marcus	A	2/Central
Northlake Mall	Charlotte, NC	Charlotte metro	Belk, Dillards	B	2/Central
Triangle Town Center	Raleigh, NC	Raleigh, NC	Saks, Macy's, Dillards	B	2/Central
The Streets at Southport	Durham, NC	Durham, NC	Nordstrom, Macy's, Hudson-Belk	B	2/Central

continued

TABLE I.3 (CONTINUED)

PERRY'S STORE LOCATIONS, RANKINGS CLUSTERS					
NAME	LOCATION	METRO AREA	ANCHORS	STORE RANK	CLUSTER
SOUTH CAROLINA (3)					
Downtown	Charleston, SC	King Street	Saks, boutiques	B	2/Central
Columbia Mall	Columbia, SC	Columbia, SC	Belk, Dillards	C	2/Central
Shelter Cove Shops	Hilton Head, SC	Shelter Cove Lane	Saks, boutiques	A	2/Central
MARYLAND (6)					
The Collection at Chevy Chase	Chevy Chase, MD	DC Metro	Saks, Neiman Marcus	A	1/Mid-Atlantic
Wisconsin Avenue	Chevy Chase, MD	DC Metro	Saks, Neiman Marcus	A	1/Mid-Atlantic
Westfield Annopolis Mall	Annapolis, MD	DC Metro	Nordstrom, Macy's	C	1/Mid-Atlantic
The Mall in Columbia	Columbia, MD	Columbia, MD	Macy's	C	1/Mid-Atlantic
Westfield Montgomery Mall	DC Metro	Bethesda, MD	Nordstrom, Macy's	C	1/Mid-Atlantic
Towson Town Center	Towson, MD	Townson, MD	Nordstrom, Macy's	B	1/Mid-Atlantic
VIRGINIA (6)					
Tysons Galleria	McLean, VA	DC Metro	Saks, Neiman Marcus, Macy's	A	1/Mid-Atlantic
Fashion Center @Pentagon City	Arlington, VA	DC Metro	Nordstrom, Bloomingdales, Macy's	B	1/Mid-Atlantic
Fredericksburg Downtown	King Street	Suburban DC	boutiques only	B	1/Mid-Atlantic
Stony Point	Richmond, VA	Central	Saks, Dillards	B	1/Mid-Atlantic
Mc Arthur Center	Virginia Beach, VA	East Coast	Nordstrom, Macy's	C	1/Mid-Atlantic
Historic District	Williamsburg, VA	Williamsburg	Boutiques only	A	1/Mid-Atlantic
WASHINGTON, DC (2)					
Mazza Gallerie	Washington, DC	DC Metro	Saks, Neiman Marcus	A	1/Mid-Atlantic
M Street	Georgetown,	DC Metro	Boutiques	A	1/Mid-Atlantic

TABLE I.4

AVERAGE STORE SALES VOLUME BY STORE RANKING			
STORES BY RANKING	**% OF TOTAL**	**SALES BY RANK**	**AVG. STORE SALES**
A stores: 16	55%	$491.7M	$30.7 M per A Store
B stores: 15	30%	$268.2 M	$17.9 M per B Store
C stores: 8	15%	$134.1 M	$16.8 M per C Store
TOTAL SALES FOR ALL STORES		$894.M	

Today, many stores also cluster their branches based on common characteristics, such as geographic region, climate, store location, seasonal considerations, and even color preferences. Of course, Florida stores would have different merchandise requirements than Maryland stores for the winter months. Another example might be that northeastern stores tend to carry more black and gray, whereas southeastern stores tend to carry a brighter palette. Some retailers use long-range weather forecasts to anticipate weather-related merchandise selling opportunities. This allows buyers to address loss sales or excessive markdowns because the right merchandise is not in the right place at the right time. Table I.5 shows how Perry's clusters or regionalizes its stores into two clusters.

TABLE I.5

PERRY'S DEPARTMENT STORE: REGIONAL CLUSTERS WITH STORE NUMBERS

CLUSTER 1: MID ATLANTIC	CLUSTER 2: CENTRAL	CLUSTER 3: FLORIDA
MARYLAND (6)	GEORGIA (5)	FLORIDA (13)

CLUSTER 1: MID ATLANTIC

MARYLAND (6)

- The Collection at Chevy Chase (C1-1)
- Wisconsin Avenue (C1-2)
- Westfield Annapolis Mall (C1-3)
- The Mall in Columbia (C1-4)
- Westfield Montgomery Mall (C1-5)
- Towson Town Center (C1-6)

VIRGINIA (6)

- Tysons Galleria (C1-7)
- Fashion Center @ Pentagon City (C1-8)
- Fredericksburg Downtown (C1-9)
- Stony Point (C1-10)
- Mc Arthur Center (C1-11)
- Williamsburg Historic District (C1-12)

WASHINGTON, DC(2)

- Mazza Gallerie (C1-13)
- M Street, Georgetown (C1-14)

CLUSTER 2: CENTRAL

GEORGIA (5)

- Savannah, GA Downtown (C2-15)
- Lenox Mall (C2-16)
- Phipps Plaza (C2-17)
- Perimeter Mall (C2-18)
- The Mall of Georgia (C2-19)

NORTH CAROLINA (4)

- South Park Mall (C2-20)
- Northlake Mall (C2-21)
- Triangle Town Center (C2-22)
- The Streets at Southport (C2-23)

SOUTH CAROLINA (3)

- Downtown Savannah (C2-24)
- Columbia Mall (C2-25)
- Shelter Cove Shops (C2-26)

CLUSTER 3: FLORIDA

FLORIDA (13)

- Aventura Mall (C3-27)
- Boca Raton Town Center (C3-28)
- Worth Avenue (C3-29)
- Galleria Fort Lauderdale (C3-30)
- Bal Harbour (C3-31)
- The Mall at Wellington Green (C3-32)
- International Plaza (C3-33)
- Bell Tower Shops (C3-34)
- Waterside Shops (C3-35)
- The Mall at Millenia (C3-36)
- Florida Mall (C3-37)
- The Falls (C3-38)
- The Gardens Mall (C3-39)

THE SIMULATION BEGINS

You have been with Perry's as an assistant buyer since graduating from college four years ago. A buying position has opened, and you have been offered the job. You have been given 60 days to reorganize and develop a step-by-step plan before your first market trip to purchase for the fall/holiday season. For the purpose of this simulation, you will need to select one of the following departments: women's contemporary, women's accessories, children's, juniors', men's contemporary, or home furnishings.

Your step-by-step plan is as follows:

STEP 1.   Redefine Perry's customer for your area
STEP 2.   Research and report on current fashion and industry trends
STEP 3.   Develop the fall/holiday six-month buying plan
STEP 4.   Develop stock assortment plans
STEP 5.   Prepare to shop the market
STEP 6.   Plan market purchases
STEP 7.   Negotiate profitability
STEP 8.   Examine the income statement

There are guidelines for each step of your plan. Remember to justify all of your conclusions, as you are being scrutinized by upper management.

## CHAPTER 1

STEP 1

Redefine Your Customer

IN THIS CHAPTER, YOU WILL LEARN:

* How to analyze statistical and psychographic information to develop a customer profile for A, B, and C stores
* What publications are used in various segments of the fashion industry

Your first assignment as a new buyer is to redefine Perry's customer for your department. Use the demographic and statistical information offered in the Introduction, as well as the new information in this chapter, to define three customer types that shop at A, B, and C stores in the Washington, DC metropolitan area, or what is called the Mid-Atlantic cluster. (Use the form shown in Figure 1.2 on page 8 to record your research.)

In addition to the demographic and statistical information supplied in the Introduction, you should conduct additional research in the area of psychographics. Perry's companion website lists links to numerous sources of consumer behavior information, such as VALS and the Lifestyle Monitor from Cotton Inc. Psychographics explores the primary motivation for an individual's purchasing behaviors or the psychology behind their buying.

VALS

Many market research organizations offer various types of psychographic information. Most of these organizations segment on the basis of consumer behaviors, attitudes, interests, or opinions. None of these measures explains why individual consumers exhibit different behaviors or why individual consumers exhibit the same behaviors for different reasons. VALS/ (Values, Attitudes, and Lifestyle Survey) provides explanations. Developed by SRI International (Menlo Park, California) and now owned and operated by Strategic Business Insights (SBI; Menlo Park, California), VALS is an eight-segment consumer framework that profiles consumers on two dimensions: primary motivation and resources.

An individual's primary motivation directs what he or she finds meaningful in the world around him or herself. The majority of consumers are driven by one of three motivations: ideals, achievement, or self-expression. How an individual acts as a consumer is the by-product of his or her motivation and the individual's available resources, such as energy, self-confidence, impulsiveness, leadership, vanity, education, and income. A proprietary algorithm determines which group an individual is most like on the basis of the individual's responses to 34 attitude questions and 4 key demographic questions in the VALS survey. Research has empirically proved the VALS attitude questions correlate most closely with consumption of merchandise (see Figure 1.1). An example of a typical question would be:

1. I follow the latest trends and fashions.

   o Mostly disagree
   o Somewhat disagree
   o Somewhat agree
   o Mostly agree

Consumer-behavior profiles for each group are the result of the VALS survey's inclusion in either proprietary client surveys or large national surveys, such as GfK Mediamark Research & Intelligence, LLC's *The Survey of the American Consumer* (see Table 1.1).

High-resource and low-resource groups exist within each of the three primary motivations (see Figure 1.1). Thinkers and Believers share an ideals motivation. Achievers and Strivers share an achievement motivation. Experiencers and Makers share a self-expression motivation. Two groups operate outside of the motivations dimension. Innovators, with the most abundant resources, display the most positive attributes of Thinkers, Achievers, and Experiencers. Survivors, with the most constrained resources, display attributes of constrained Believers, Strivers, or Makers.

Because Perry's is an upscale department store, only the four high-resource VALS groups—Innovators, Thinkers, Achievers, and Experiencers—are potential customers. Table 1.1 allows you to compare and contrast the groups quickly.

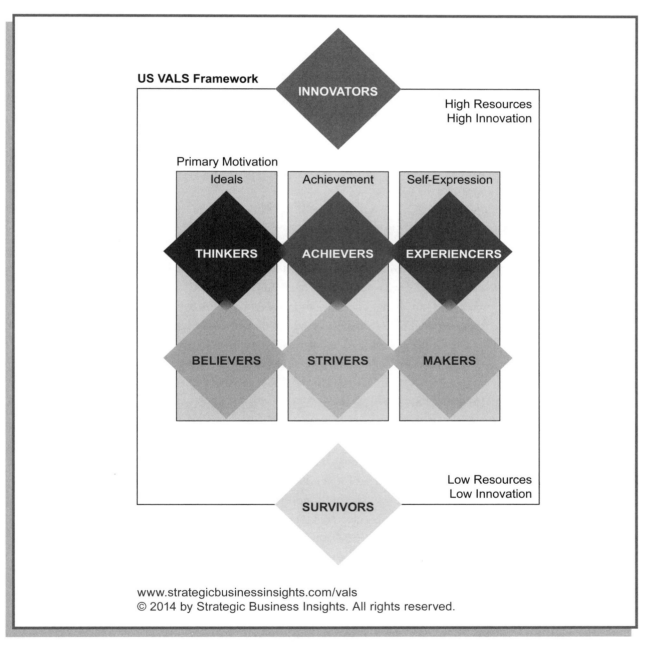

FIGURE 1.1 VALS types

VALS SEGMENT DESCRIPTIONS

Innovators are successful, sophisticated, take-charge people with high self-confidence and self-esteem. They are change leaders and are the most receptive to new ideas and technologies. Their purchases reflect cultivated tastes for upscale, niche products, services, brands, and retailers.

IDEALS MOTIVATION

Thinkers are mature, satisfied, comfortable, and reflective. They tend to be well educated and actively seek out information in the buying decision-making process. They favor durability, functionality, and value in products.

Believers are strongly traditional and respect rules and authority. Because they are fundamentally conservative, they are slow to change and technology laggards. They choose familiar products and established brands, and they shop at retailers whose personnel know them by name.

ACHIEVEMENT MOTIVATION

Achievers are goal oriented and center on family and career. They avoid situations that encourage a high degree of stimulation or change. They prefer premium products and brands that demonstrate success to their peers.

Strivers are trendy and fun loving. They have little discretionary income and tend to have narrow interests. They favor stylish products that emulate the purchases of people with greater material wealth. Many Strivers believe that life isn't fair and that they're entitled to what people with more money have.

SELF-EXPRESSION MOTIVATION

Experiencers appreciate the unconventional. They are active and impulsive, seeking stimulation from the new and offbeat. They spend a comparatively high proportion of their discretionary dollars on clothing, technology, and entertainment.

Makers value practicality and self-sufficiency. They choose hands-on constructive activities and spend leisure time with family and close friends. Because they prefer value to luxury, they buy basic products. Makers prefer to "buy American."

Survivors lead narrowly focused lives. Because they have the fewest resources, they do not exhibit a primary motivation; they often feel powerless and forgotten. Concerned about safety and security, they are brand and retail-channel loyal as long as they can afford to be so.

TABLE 1.1

HIGH-RESOURCE VALS GROUP COMPARISON				
VALS GROUP	**INNOVATORS**	**THINKERS**	**ACHIEVERS**	**EXPERIENCERS**
Percent of US adults	10	11	14	13
Mean Age	47	58	43	25
Median HHI	$128K	$109K	$109K	$70K
CHARACTERISTICS	SOPHISTICATED, IN CHARGE, CURIOUS CONTENT	INFORMED, REFLECTIVE, CONVENTIONAL	ME FIRST, BRAND CONSCIOUS, VARIETY SEEKING	TREND SETTING, SPONTANEOUS,
	(PERCENT)	(PERCENT)	(PERCENT)	(PERCENT)
Women	46	51	57	43
Married	60	72	72	22
Caucasian	89	88	80	60
Children under age 18 in HH	31	26	50	55
Live with parents/relative	6	1	10	44
Employed full-time	62	49	66	40
Spent $2000+ on clothing in past 12 months	7	3	5	8
Bought 3+ items of women's clothing in past 12 months	45	45	50	41
Bought 3+ items of men's clothing in past 12 months	53	51	47	48
Spent $250+ on shoes in past 12 months	17	10	11	12
Shop Nordstrom in past 3 months	16	7	6	5
Shop Marshalls in past 3 months	12	12	14	15
Are HENRYs	56	44	47	22

Table reads: 46% of Innovators are women, 60% of Innovators are married, 7% of Innovators spent $2000 or more on clothing in the past 12 months.

Source: VALS//GfK MRI Spring 2013

SIMULATION

Go to www.strategicbusinessinsights.com/vals/presurvey.shtml.

Take the VALS survey and report your personal profile to your division merchandising manager (DMM). Buyers must be careful not to purchase merchandise based on their own taste and buying preference rather than that of their departmental customer. If you understand your own buying motivations, you are less likely to confuse them with those of the Perry's customer.

By design, the questions are for use by people whose first language is American English. If you are not a citizen of the United States or Canada, residency should be for enough time to know the culture and its idioms. If you do not meet these conditions, your VALS type will not be valid.

VALS also offers additional research to enable users to profile geography by the concentrations of consumer groups. GeoVALS estimates the percent distribution of each of the VALS groups by counties and zip codes. GeoVALS provides a retail buyer with key target consumer information for his or her trading area. GeoVALS is a method to estimate potential sales performance by location and define the merchandise mix based on the concentration of the consumer segment. SBI provides GeoVALS data on the website for your use in developing your consumer profile.

Additional information about luxury consumer profiles is available in your university library. Conducting additional research about luxury consumers will improve your decisions as a buyer and help support the information you provide in your project.

CULTURAL DIFFERENCES

With the constant shifting of demographics in metropolitan and suburban areas of the United States, retail buyers must be in tune with the cultural changes in their marketplace. For example, if a shift in population indicates a significant increase in the number of Latino consumers, then a buyer must understand the implications of a multicultural marketplace. According to Fox News Latino, U.S upscale Latinos earning $110,000 plus have increased 221 percent in the last decade, and this segment is growing 8 percent faster than other ethnic segments (Gil, 2013). Using this example, it would benefit a buyer (and his or her company) to find the styles and brands that young Latinos prefer. You should also consider whether there are any differences in color or style preferences or size ranges based on culture and ethnicity. To read this article in full, go to this link: http://latino.foxnews.com/latino/opinion/2013/06/11 /five-reasons-why-upscale-latinos-represent-next-market-boom/.

SIMULATION

Refer to the Perry's website for the GeoVALS information to secure demographic and statistical data and to obtain appropriate publications for your research. You will also find "Snapshots" or profiles of VALS buying behaviors for the segments that are most likely to shop at Perry's. With this information and additional research, complete three worksheets in Figure 1.2, one each for an A, B, and C store assortment in the Mid-Atlantic Cluster. (See Worksheet 1 on the Perry's website.)

* *Your consumer profiles should include the following information:*
* *Average age of purchaser (not necessarily consumer as in children's wear)*
* *Mean family income and median household income*
* *GeoVALS profile*
* *Buying behaviors that are both cognitive and emotional, such as purchasing quality, perfectionism, conspicuous consumption, exclusivity, or prestige*
* *Cultural and regional implications*
* *Key fashion brands for each consumer profile*

____ **Store Ranking for Mid Atlantic Cluster**

Average Age of Purchaser:

_____

Mean Family Income:

_____

Median Household Income:

_____

VALS Profile Characteristics

Buying Behaviors for Perry's consumer based VALS segments, GEO VALS and other consumer buying behavior research

Cultural and Regional Implications and Influences

Key Fashion Brands worn by this consumer (per department)

FIGURE 1.2 Perry's consumer profile worksheet

## CHAPTER 2

STEP 2

Research Current Market and Fashion Trends

IN THIS CHAPTER, YOU WILL LEARN:

⋆ The type of information buyers need to become experts in their industry/market
⋆ The resources used to research various fashion and giftware industries

Your next step is to become an authority on your industry as quickly as possible. This involves researching current fashion trends, industry characteristics, and business news.

Numerous global resources provide retail buyers, manufacturers, designers, marketing agencies, and public relations firms with fashion industry, market, and trend information. Two online subscription-based fashion forecasting firms are WGSN and Fashion Snoops. They offer an abundance of worldwide information on trend analysis, industry news, *trade shows*, speed-to-market, new designers, brands, retailers and manufacturers, and product development efficiencies. Markets covered include women's wear, menswear, children's wear, fashion accessories, beauty, vintage, and interior/home fashion. These service-based companies are based in fashion capitals such as New York City, Paris, or London, with international satellite offices in Japan, China, Australia, Brazil, and numerous other locations around the world. Because these websites are subscription only, as a student you will not be able to access all of the market and trend information. However, check with your school library to see if they have a subscription. WGSN has a monthly newsletter that does *not* require a subscription. Many *trade publications* and business publications also offer information on fashion trends and retail benchmarks to provide guidance and direction to the retail buyer. A few sources include the following:

TRADE PUBLICATIONS

Business of Fashion: http://www.businessoffashion.com/

California Apparel News: http://www.apparelnews.net/

Chain Store Age: http://www.chainstoreage.com/

Daily News Record: www.dnrnews.com

Earnshaws: http://www.earnshaws.com/

Fibre to Fashion: http://www.fibre2fashion.com/

Home Furnishings News (HFN): http://www.hfnmag.com/

InfoMat Fashion: http://fashion.infomat.com/

Just-Style: http://www.just-style.com/

National Retail Federation: www.nrf.com/RetailHeadlines

Stores Magazine: https://nrf.com/connect-us/stores-magazine

We Connect Fashion: http://weconnectfashion.com/

Women's Wear Daily (WWD): http://www.wwd.com/

*See Appendix A and the website for a more extensive list of sources for industry information.

BUSINESS PUBLICATIONS

Business Week

Forbes

Fortune

New York Times Style Section

Wall Street Journal

Industry characteristics cover information particular to a market. A buyer must know what categories of merchandise and sizes are pertinent for his or her department. For example, the junior women's buyer knows that jeans run by waist size (e.g., 25, 26, 27, 28), whereas the women's buyer probably buys jeans in a traditional size range (e.g., 4, 6, 8). This is the same for market dates and trade show locations. It may be crucial for a young men's buyer to travel to the MAGIC show, which is held in Las Vegas every February and August, but for a home furnishings buyer, the Atlanta trade shows held in January and July are the most important. In the women's apparel industry, purchase terms of 8/10 EOM (end of the month) may be quoted, whereas terms of net 30 would be quoted in the tabletop market.

Does the buyer of a particular area travel domestically only or internationally as well? What percentage of his or her department's merchandise is regular-priced and what percentage is promotional, if any? What proportion of the merchandise selection should be fashion-forward or basic? Certain brands may be vital to set the status of the department. Is private label merchandise carried and, if so, who develops the brand for each department?

Industry statistics are included on the Perry's Department Store website. Other good sources for obtaining information include interviews with:

* Retail store buyers or assistant buyers

* Retail store department managers

* Manufacturer sales representatives

THE FASHION OFFICE

A good buyer is always searching for new trends that will produce a strong sell-through with excellent margins for his or her department. Preplanning often begins at the fashion office within the department store. This division of the department store acts as the visionary for the entire store, providing a centralized visual and merchandise direction for all departments within the organization. The fashion director is the individual who leads the fashion office and is responsible for narrowing down trends from fashion shows and determining specific items and looks that should be emphasized in the entire store. The role of the fashion director may include the expansion of shops of highly profitable designers and the oversight of the visual merchandising to present a cohesive image or look for the entire department store. The fashion office provides buyers with market and fashion trend advice, as well as many other services.

Some of the services the fashion office might provide for the buyer are:

* Reports on market and fashion trends

* Assistance with six-month dollar and merchandise assortment plans

* Introduction to new resources

* Exclusivity of merchandise (private label and special purchases)

* Arrangement of vendor appointments

* Vendor Look Books

You can find an example of a trend and market report from a fashion office on the Perry's website.

THE BUYING AND MERCHANDISE FLOW CALENDAR

Figure 2.1 provides you with a buying calendar to illustrate how seasonal purchases and delivery dates are designated by the market. This calendar may vary slightly year by year and should be verified through research about market dates.

PERRY'S

APPAREL BUYING CALENDAR AND MERCHANDISE FLOW

MONTH	MARKET	DELIVERY	EVENTS
January	Summer	March April May	Vacation
March	Transitional Early Fall	June July	Back-to-School
May	Fall September	August Fall/Holiday Promotions	Holiday Catalogs
August	Holiday Cruise Early Spring	October November December January	After-Christmas Promotions
October	Spring	January February	Easter

FIGURE 2.1 Perry's buying calendar

Using a minimum of five sources, write and submit a report on your specific industry. Your report should be in outline form, covering the following topics and format:

1. Market dates and delivery timeline for the upcoming year

2. Market and trade show locations

3. Characteristics unique to the industry, such as sizing, prepack purchasing, sourcing

4. Typical terms of purchase

5. Lead time on both domestic and foreign goods after market date

6. Cooperative advertising agreements (bill enclosures, magazine, etc.)

7. Off-price and promotional merchandise availability

8. Fashion trends in:
   a. Classifications
   b. Subclassifications
   c. Colors
   d. Fabrications/material
   e. Prints and patterns
   f. Silhouettes

9. Major vendors for each classification

10. Market trends (imports, licensed characters, etc.)

## CHAPTER 3

STEP 3

Develop Buying Plan

IN THIS CHAPTER, YOU WILL LEARN:

* To prepare a six-month merchandise plan
* The concept behind the 4-5-4 calendar
* To become confident in estimating plan figures
* To analyze last year's figures and competitive operating results
* To calculate open-to-buy

Now that you have obtained significant knowledge and background information about your industry, it is time to prepare your merchandise plan. The most common merchandise plan is for a six-month period. The purpose of this plan is to budget your dollars that will be spent on merchandise in relation to your projected sales. The goal of every department is to plan the right merchandise in the right quantity at the right price in the right place at the right time.

The *six-month merchandise plan* concentrates on the right quantity at the right price at the proper time. It plans merchandise in dollars, not by style or color.

Although the plan format may vary from one retail organization to another, the components remain the same. These components are:

1. Planned sales

2. Planned beginning-of-the-month (BOM) stock

3. Planned markdowns

4. Planned purchases

Note that there are many different formats for six-month plans, usually designed by the individual store. Figure 3.1 shows Perry's six-month August through January

SEASON: FALL		AUGUST	SEPTEMBER	OCTOBER	NOVEMBER	DECEMBER	JANUARY	FEBRUARY	SEASON TOTAL
SALES ($ in mil)	Last Year	$ 3.7	$ 3.6	$ 3.7	$ 4.6	$ 7.0	$ 2.5		$ 25.1
	Plan	$ 3.9	$ 3.7	$ 3.9	$ 4.8	$ 7.2	$ 2.6		$ 26.1
	% Inc/Dec	5.4%	2.8%	5.4%	4.3%	2.9%	4.0%		4.0%
	Revised								
	Actual								
STOCK/SALES RATIO	Last Year	2.1	2.1	2.2	1.8	1.8	2.4		
	Plan	1.9	1.9	2.1	1.6	1.6	2.2		
BOM STOCK $ ($ in mil)	Last Year	$ 7.9	$ 7.7	$ 8.2	$ 8.3	$ 12.5	$ 6.0	$ 6.1	AV STOCK $ 8.1
	Plan	$ 7.3	$ 7.1	$7.6	$7.7	$ 11.6	$ 5.6	$ 5.6	$ 7.5
	Revised								
	Actual								
MARKDOWNS $ ($ in mil)	Last Year	$ 1.9	$ 1.0	$1.4	$ 1.1	$ 2.8	$ 1.3		$ 9.5
	Plan	$ 1.8	$ 0.9	$1.4	$ 1.1	$ 2.8	$ 1.4		$ 9.4
	% to Sales	46.2%	24.3%	35.9%	22.9%	38.9%	53.8%		36.0%
	% by Month	19.1%	9.6%	14.9%	11.7%	29.8%	14.9%		100.0%
	Revised								
	Actual								
PURCHASES $ ($ in mil)	Last Year	$ 5.4	$ 5.1	$ 5.2	$ 9.9	$ 3.3	$ 3.9		$ 32.8
	Plan	$ 5.5	$ 5.1	$ 5.4	$ 9.8	$ 4.0	$ 4.0		$ 33.8
	Revised								
	Actual								

SEASON TOT.	LAST YEAR	PLAN	ACTUAL
Sales ($ in mil)	$25.1	$26.1	
Markup %	53%	54%	
Markdown %	38%	36%	
Gross Margin %	35.1%	37.4%	
Average Stock	$8.1	$7.5	
Turnover	3.1	3.48	
NOTES:			

FIGURE 3.1 Perry's juniors' department fall six-month dollar plan

merchandise plan for the junior apparel department. A junior apparel department example will be used throughout the simulation, but students may choose any of Perry's listed departments to research. See Perry's website for a blank six-month plan.

As with any budget, the six-month plan is a guideline to help the buyer spend dollars wisely. The objectives are to:

1. Decrease dollars invested in inventory

2. Increase turnover (number of times merchandise is restocked in a given period)

3. Control open-to-buy (money available to purchase additional merchandise)

4. Allow for improvement over last year's figures

5. Reduce loss of sales due to understocked merchandise

6. Improve gross margin

7. Provide a point of reference for comparing actual results to planned performance

The merchandise plan is developed in advance of the selling season, usually for a six-month period, for either the spring/summer or fall/holiday season. Perry's plan coincides with the retail-accounting calendar, or the 4-5-4 calendar, used by many department stores and retail operations. Figure 3.2 is an example of a 4-5-4 calendar. This retail-accounting or fiscal calendar provides continuity by expressing seasons in "comparative selling" weeks and months.

The 4-5-4 calendar begins with February and segments each quarter into three periods—four weeks in period I, five weeks in period II, and four weeks in period III—hence the name 4-5-4 calendar. For example, in the first quarter, February is four weeks, March is five weeks, and April is four weeks. Each month begins on Sunday and ends on Saturday. Breaking down the quarters into standard periods allows a retailer to forecast more accurately and to compare figures against the same period from one year to the next, since accounting periods stay the same from year to year. You will note that adjusting the calendar in this manner may result in the shifting of days from one month to another for accounting purposes. Another benefit of using the 4-5-4 calendar is that it follows the flow of retail business. For example, the spring season for the retailer is typically February through April, or the first quarter of the 4-5-4 calendar. The Julian calendar that we follow daily begins the year with January, which does not align with the beginning of the retail spring season. Despite the benefits of using the 4-5-4 calendar, many retail businesses still use the Julian calendar.

SPRING SEASON   2015   FALL SEASON

FIRST QUARTER

FEBRUARY

WK		S	M	T	W	T	F	S
1	1	1	2	3	4	5	6	7
2	2	8	9	10	11	12	13	14
3	3	15	16	17	18	19	20	21
4	4	22	23	24	25	26	27	28

MARCH

WK		S	M	T	W	T	F	S
5	1	1	2	3	4	5	6	7
6	2	8	9	10	11	12	13	14
7	3	15	16	17	18	19	20	21
8	4	22	23	24	25	26	27	28
9	5	29	30	31	1	2	3	4

APRIL

WK		S	M	T	W	T	F	S
10	1	5	6	7	8	9	10	11
11	2	12	13	14	15	16	17	18
12	3	19	20	21	22	23	24	25
13	4	26	27	28	29	30	1	2

THIRD QUARTER

AUGUST

	S	M	T	W	T	F	S	WK
1	2	3	4	5	6	7	8	27
2	9	10	11	12	13	14	15	28
3	16	17	18	19	20	21	22	29
4	23	24	25	26	27	28	29	30

SEPTEMBER

	S	M	T	W	T	F	S	WK
1	30	31	1	2	3	4	5	31
2	6	7	8	9	10	11	12	32
3	13	14	15	16	17	18	19	33
4	20	21	22	23	24	25	26	34
5	27	28	29	30	1	2	3	35

OCTOBER

	S	M	T	W	T	F	S	WK
1	4	5	6	7	8	9	10	36
2	11	12	13	14	15	16	17	37
3	18	19	20	21	22	23	24	38
4	25	26	27	28	29	30	31	39

SECOND QUARTER

MAY

WK		S	M	T	W	T	F	S
14	1	3	4	5	6	7	8	9
15	2	10	11	12	13	14	15	16
16	3	17	18	19	20	21	22	23
17	4	24	25	26	27	28	29	30

JUNE

WK		S	M	T	W	T	F	S
18	1	5	6	7	8	9	10	11
19	2	12	13	14	15	16	17	18
20	3	19	20	21	22	23	24	25
21	4	22	23	24	25	26	27	28
22	5	29	30	31	1	2	3	4

JULY

WK		S	M	T	W	T	F	S
23	1	5	6	7	8	9	10	11
24	2	12	13	14	15	16	17	18
25	3	19	20	21	22	23	24	25
26	4	26	27	28	29	30	31	1

FOURTH QUARTER

NOVEMBER

	S	M	T	W	T	F	S	WK
1	1	2	3	4	5	6	7	40
2	8	9	10	11	12	13	14	41
3	15	16	17	18	19	20	21	42
4	22	23	24	25	26	27	28	43

DECEMBER

	S	M	T	W	T	F	S	WK
1	29	30	1	2	3	4	5	44
2	6	7	8	9	10	11	12	45
3	13	14	15	16	17	18	19	46
4	20	21	22	23	24	25	26	47
5	27	28	29	30	31	1	2	48

JANUARY 2016

	S	M	T	W	T	F	S	WK
1	3	4	5	6	7	8	9	49
2	10	11	12	13	14	15	16	50
3	17	18	19	20	21	22	23	51
4	24	25	26	27	28	29	30	52

FIGURE 3.2 Fiscal year 2015 4-5-4 accounting calendar

Perry's six-month merchandise plan follows the 4-5-4 calendar, with two six-month periods, February through July and August through January. Each season has 26 weeks, or two 13-week quarters.

Planned sales are the most significant element of the buyer's plan, because they are the basis for all other elements of the entire budgeting process (BOM stock, markdowns, etc.). Starting with past sales history, the buyer uses his or her experience, market knowledge, and research to make accurate sales forecasts. Research is a necessary component of forecasting and should include:

1. Previous year's sales performance

2. Local, regional, and national economic information

3. Sales trends

4. Fashion trends

5. Competition

Considering these factors, a buyer (with input from upper management) might forecast a sales increase or decrease, or for sales to remain "flat" (maintaining the same amount of sales as the previous year's season).

EXAMPLE:

After considering an inflation factor of 2% and local income growth of 2%, a buyer determines a 4% increase in sales over last year's sales total of $25.0 million. What would the projected sales be for the next year?

$$
\begin{array}{rr}
\$25{,}000{,}000 & \$25{,}000{,}000 \\
\times \qquad .04 & + \quad 1{,}000{,}000 \\
\hline
\$\,1{,}000{,}000 & \$26{,}000{,}000 \\
\end{array}
$$

A simple one-step formula can be used to determine the sales increase:

Last Year Sales × (1 + Planned %) = Planned Sales
$25,000,000 × (1 + .04) = $26,000,000

The buyer's next step is to break down this sales increase by month for the six-month period.

For example, if planning for August through January, the buyer would plan for sales to increase, decrease, or to remain flat for each month.

Estimating is not an exact science. After a buyer considers all possible factors that could impact the business, he or she makes an educated guess. There is no one right answer. A group of buyers, given the same past history and current information, are likely to arrive at different forecasts based on individual perceptions and interpretations. As long as the buyer can justify the forecast, management is likely to approve the figures.

PLANNING SALES

Your first step in planning your budget is to select one of Perry's departments and determine your sales for the fall/holiday six-month period, August through January. Retail stores belonging to a buying group or office are provided with the past year's statistics from member stores. Buyers can compare their department's performance related to stock turnover, stock-to-sales ratios, monthly sales distribution, markdowns, and so on, with both median and par performances of other comparable stores. Not all stores belong to a buying group or office. For Perry's department store, a good reference is to research the annual report (10K) of similar stores to compare performance. Figure 3.3 shows Perry's company merchandise operating results for a year.

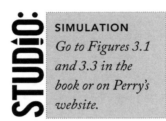

STUDIO:

SIMULATION
Go to Figures 3.1 and 3.3 in the book or on Perry's website.

A two-year total sales history is shown for the total company and seven key departments. Choose one of the seven departments to develop a six-month plan. Additional sales information for each department can be found on Perry's website.

The factors you should consider in planning your six-month budget are:

1. Sales history of the department for the six-month period of the past year (refer to Figures 3.1 and 3.3 in the textbook or on the website)

2. Industry statistics

3. Fashion trends

4. Local, national, and regional economics

5. Buying office or fashion office market report

You will need to research current economic indicators on retail growth to obtain information to estimate your department's sales growth. Perry's website lists suggested websites to research economic indicators. Use the current information you find to assist you in making an educated forecast regarding how much you might expect your departmental sales to increase or decrease for your six-month plan.

Use Figure 3.4 in the textbook or on Perry's website to record your total department sales plan for the six-month period, justifying your sales increase or

PERRY'S

PERRY'S MERCHANDISE OPERATING RESULTS

$ in millions

Sales Data	Total Store	Women's Contemporary Apparel	Junior Apparel	Women's Accessories	Men's Apparel & Accessories	Men's Contemporary Apparel	Children's	Home Furnishings	Other
This Year Sales	$ 894.0	$ 259.3	$ 44.7	$ 116.2	$ 107.3	$ 35.8	$ 26.8	$ 53.6	$ 250.3
Previous Year Sales	$ 864.5	$ 248.1	$ 43.6	$ 109.6	$ 104.2	$ 34.4	$ 26.2	$ 51.8	$ 246.6
Net Sales % Change from Previous Year	3.4%	4.5%	2.5%	6%	3%	4.1%	2.3%	3.5%	1.5%
Net Sales % of Total Store	100%	29%	5%	13%	12%	4%	3%	6%	28%
Merchandising & Inventory									
Cumulative Markup %	53.6%	53.3%	53.1%	54.9%	52.7%	53.7%	52.3%	55%	53.5%
Markdown %	27.0%	35.2%	37.7%	18.2%	27.9%	29.2%	30%	25%	20%
Stock Shortage %	2.2%	2.3%	2.6%	3.2%	2.3%	2.7%	1.9%	2.2%	1.6%
Gross Margin % (w/ Workroom Cost & Cash Discount)	39.2%	35.1%	35.4%	45.0%	38.2%	39.6%	38.2%	42.0%	45.8%
Inventory Productivity									
Stock Turnover	3.0	3.5	3.1	2.1	2.3	2.4	2.9	2.1	2.8

Total Company Monthly Sales Distribution %

	FEBRUARY	MARCH	APRIL	MAY	JUNE	JULY	AUGUST	SEPTEMBER	OCTOBER	NOVEMBER	DECEMBER	JANUARY	TOTAL
	6.4%	8.2%	7.4%	7.6%	7.7%	6.7%	8.2%	8.0%	8.3%	10.3%	15.6%	5.6%	100%
$	57.2	73.3	66.2	67.9	68.8	59.9	73.3	71.5	74.2	92.1	139.5	50.1	894.0

Total Company Monthly Markdowns % To Sales

	FEBRUARY	MARCH	APRIL	MAY	JUNE	JULY	AUGUST	SEPTEMBER	OCTOBER	NOVEMBER	DECEMBER	JANUARY	TOTAL
	29.5%	26.7%	24.5%	20.9%	28.5%	33.1%	28.0%	24.3%	25.3%	22.3%	24.2%	48.1%	28%
$	16.9	19.6	16.2	14.2	19.6	19.8	20.5	17.4	18.8	20.5	33.8	24.1	241.4

Total Company Stock to Sales Ratio

	FEBRUARY	MARCH	APRIL	MAY	JUNE	JULY	AUGUST	SEPTEMBER	OCTOBER	NOVEMBER	DECEMBER	JANUARY
	5.1	4.2	4.5	4.4	4.2	4.9	4	4.3	4.4	3.6	2.1	5.2
$	291.7	307.9	297.9	298.8	289.0	293.5	293.2	307.5	326.5	331.6	293.0	260.5

FIGURE 3.3 Perry's merchandise operating results

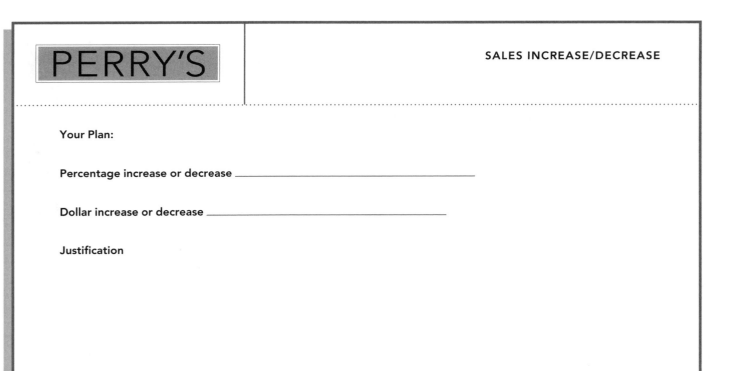

Your Plan:

Percentage increase or decrease _____

Dollar increase or decrease _____

Justification

FIGURE 3.4 Perry's sales plan worksheet

decrease for your department based on your research. Remember that the fall/holiday season does a greater percentage of business than the spring/summer period because of several factors, including shopping-intensive periods such as back-to-school, Christmas, and other holidays.

Once you have justified your sales increase or decrease, your next step is to break down your sales by month. Your considerations will be:

1. Last year's actual sales distribution (percentage of sales obtained each month in relation to season total)

2. Retail-accounting calendar, with adjustments for holidays and special promotions

3. Recommendations from Perry's buying office in monthly sales distribution (in percentages) for the upcoming fall/holiday season

You can see Perry's total store sales distribution percentage for an entire year in Figure 3.3. You may also refer to the sales distribution for the juniors' department in Figure 3.1 for a fall/holiday season and use this percentage of distribution as your guideline. Each department within a store varies in percentage of distribution. For example, the children's department would have a higher percentage of sales in August and September due to back-to-school shopping. Store special events and sales would also affect sales in a department for a particular month. You may use the Perry's sales distribution as listed in Figures 3.1 and 3.3 and on the website, or vary the percentages based on your research and plan. Remember, this is a forecast, and there is not one correct answer. Perry's total company sales distribution percentage by six-month periods from Figure 3.3 is as follows:

February	14.54%
March	18.64%
April	16.83%
May	17.26%
June	17.50%
July	15.23%
TOTAL	100%

August	14.64%
September	14.28%
October	14.82%
November	18.39%
December	27.86%
January	10.01%
TOTAL	100%

Using Figure 3.5 in the textbook or on Perry's website, start by filling in your department last year sales and sales distribution for the six-month period of August through January. Next, plan your monthly sales distribution and determine your plan sales by month. Calculate the dollar and percentage of increase or decrease of planned sales in relation to last year's actual figures. At the bottom of the worksheet, make notes to justify the reasons for your sales forecast by month.

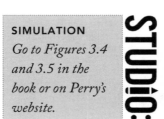

SIMULATION
Go to Figures 3.4 and 3.5 in the book or on Perry's website.

STUDIO:

	AUGUST	SEPTEMBER	OCTOBER	NOVEMBER	DECEMBER	JANUARY	Total
PL Sales							
% by Month							100%
LY Sales							
% by Month							100%
$ Inc/Dec							
% Inc/Dec							

Justification by Month:

August

September

October

November

December

January

FIGURE 3.5 Perry's monthly sales plan and increase/decrease

PLANNING BEGINNING-OF-THE-MONTH STOCK (BOM STOCK)

A buyer plans a beginning-of-the-month (BOM) stock sufficient to meet planned sales without overstocking the department. This is called a ***balanced stock***. Too much inventory could result in excessive markdowns and less profit. Too little inventory may result in lower sales. BOM inventory is used instead of end-of-the-month (EOM) stock, because the BOM stock produces that month's sales. For example, January BOM stock is December's EOM stock. In other words, at 11:59 PM on December 31, the stock on the sales floor (December EOM) has the same value in dollars as on January 1 at 12:01 AM (January BOM).

There are several methods of planning inventories, but the one most widely seen in the industry and taught in classrooms is the stock-to-sales ratio method. This method establishes a relationship or ratio of (BOM) stock required to meet projected sales on a monthly basis. For example, a buyer might determine from past records that in November there is a 4-to-1 ratio (expressed 4.0). That is, for every $1.00 of planned sales, $4.00 is needed in merchandise in order to achieve planned sales. The ratios will vary from month to month according to selling seasons, holidays, and so forth. Buyers consider these factors in establishing monthly stock-to-sales ratios:

* Department's previous performance

* Industry stock-to-sales ratios

After the stock-to-sales ratio or relationship is established, the buyer multiplies this ratio times the planned sales to find the BOM inventory needs in dollars.

EXAMPLE:

January planned sales = $10,000,000

Stock-to-sales ratio = 3.7

Planned sales × stock-to-sales ratio = BOM stock

$10,000,000 × 3.7 = $37,000,000 January BOM stock

If BOM stock and sales are established, use the following formula to determine the stock-to-sales ratio:

$$\frac{\text{January BOM stock}}{\text{January planned sales}} = \text{stock-to-sales ratio} = \frac{\$37,000,000}{\$10,000,000} = 3.7$$

Another method of planning inventory is ***weeks of supply***. Using this method, BOM stock is determined by adding sales for a specified number of weeks. For example, a company may plan BOM to equal the following two months of sales to provide sufficient inventory to achieve planned sales. Using this method of calculating stock, for the month of February, BOM would equal the sum of planned sales for March and April. For the month of March, BOM would equal the sum of planned sales for April and May.

Departments offering basic stock—or items that are carried throughout the year and planned to never be out of stock, such as men's button-down shirts, basic socks, or underwear—may use a different method of planning inventory. For basic stock items, a specific level of inventory to maintain is often planned, along with a specific reorder quantity once the inventory falls below the required level. Basic stock programs are often planned by store. For example, an A store inventory plan for a blue, button-down, long-sleeved shirt in a specific neck and sleeve size may be to maintain a minimum inventory level of 12 units at all times. A reorder minimum buy from the manufacturer may be 6 units. Whenever sales causes the inventory level to come close to or drop below 12 units, a reorder of 6 units is automatically placed. If the store has 18 units of the shirt in stock and plans to sell 12 units for the current month, then that would leave only 6 units in stock. A buy of 6 units would bring the inventory back to 12, but if the next month's plan is to sell another 12 units, then the reorder placed should be 6 units plus 12 units, for a total of 18 units, to ensure the level of inventory is maintained at 12 units.

TURNOVER

Turnover is the ratio of sales to average stock. Turnover is generally calculated for a season or year and used in performance analysis.

Turnover is significant to the buyer because it is a gauge of a department's efficiency and productivity. The buyer seeks a healthy turnover because it:

1. Ensures the influx of new, fresh merchandise

2. Lowers markdowns

3. Increases available dollars to purchase new merchandise (open-to-buy)

As a buyer, you can improve Perry's turnover rate by two direct methods: (1) increase sales or (2) decrease dollars invested in merchandise. This relationship is expressed as indicated in the formula for turnover:

$$\text{Stock turnover} = \frac{\text{Net sales for a period}}{\text{Average inventory or stock for the same period}}$$

Refer to Figure 3.1 Perry's juniors' department to apply the formula and determine turnover.

$$\frac{\$26,100,000 \text{ (Plan sales for August through January)}}{\$7,500,000 \text{ (Plan BOM for 6 months + EOM for January/7)}} = 3.48 \text{ Turnover}$$

Turnover for basic stock programs is a slower rate because of maintained in-stock levels throughout the year. Turnover for seasonal merchandise, such as Christmas or swimwear, is a higher rate because this type of merchandise is in and out during the particular season, and not carried throughout the year. A high rate of turnover, unless it is for seasonal merchandise that is in and out of stock in a short period of time, may indicate that inventory is too low and that sales may have been missed.

Average stock is merely the sum of the retail inventories divided by the number of inventories in the period examined (month, season, or year). The formula is:

$$\text{Average Stock} = \frac{\text{BOM stock for the given period}}{\text{\# of inventories (BOM stock)}}$$

EXAMPLE:

The average inventory for a year would be calculated by adding the 12 BOM inventories (February to January) plus the January EOM inventory, and then dividing this by 13 (the number of inventories examined).

February BOM	$ 9,350,000
March BOM	$ 9,600,000
April BOM	$ 11,550,000
May BOM	$ 12,600,000
June BOM	$ 11,400,000
July BOM	$ 11,400,000
August BOM	$ 11,550,000
September BOM	$ 12,750,000
October BOM	$ 12,300,000
November BOM	$ 13,350,000
December BOM	$ 20,100,000
January BOM	$ 13,300,000
January EOM/ (February BOM)	$ 9,650,000
TOTAL	$ 158,900,000

$$\frac{\$158,900,000}{13} = \$12,223,076.90 = \$12,223,077 \text{ (rounded off)}$$

To calculate average stock for the fall/holiday six-month period using the same example, add August BOM through January BOM stocks plus January EOM (February BOM), given as follows, and divide by 7 (the number of inventories).

EXAMPLE:

Sum of August BOM through January EOM = $93,000,000

$$\frac{\$93,000,000}{7} = \$13,285,714.30 = \$13,285,714 \text{ (rounded off)}$$

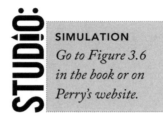

SIMULATION
Go to Figure 3.6 in the book or on Perry's website.

The next step in completing your six-month plan is to plan your stock using the stock-to-sales ratio method. First, establish your stock-to-sales ratios for each month for your department and then multiply your planned sales for each corresponding month by the stock-to-sales ratio. Remember, your possible sources of information are previous departmental performance and industry stock-to-sales ratios.

Refer to Figures 3.1 and 3.3 and Perry's website for last year's figures. Use Figure 3.6 to record your stock-to-sales ratios and BOM stock. Justify the plan stock-to-sales ratios by month.

When using the stock-to-sales ratio method of planning stock, buyers often experience difficulty in arriving at the exact planned average stock. For this reason, some buyers prefer to distribute stock by month on a percentage-to-month basis. The season's average stock figure times 7 (number of inventories) equals 100 percent of the inventory. Each month is assigned a percentage of the total based on previous years' figures. For the purpose of this simulation, you have been provided only last year's figures.

EXAMPLE USING FIGURE 3.1 JUNIORS' DEPARTMENT PLAN STOCK:

Sum of 7 months of stock = $52,000,000

August BOM stock = $7,300,000

$$\frac{\text{Month stock}}{\text{Sum of 7 months stock}} = \text{Month \% to total stock}$$

$$\frac{\$7,300,000}{\$52,000,000} = .14 \text{ or } 14\% \text{ of the total stock}$$

	AUGUST	SEPTEMBER	OCTOBER	NOVEMBER	DECEMBER	JANUARY	FEBRUARY
PL Sales							
S/S Ratio							
BOM Stock							

Plan Sales × Stock/Sales Ratio = BOM Stock

Justification by Month:

August

September

October

November

December

January

February (January EOM)

FIGURE 3.6 Perry's worksheet for stock/sales ratio and BOM stock

PLANNING MARKDOWNS

Markdowns are reductions in the retail price—a very necessary and inevitable element in fashion merchandising. They are multifunctional and a component of the six-month plan that a buyer must anticipate. The positive functions of markdowns are to:

1. Adjust pricing errors

2. Increase stock turnover

3. Correct buying errors

4. Remove out-of-season and/or broken assortment merchandise

5. Increase open-to-buy dollars (to allow the purchase of new merchandise)

6. Improve cash flow

7. Increase traffic within a store or department

These are the positive effects of markdowns, but the negative effects cannot be overlooked. These negative aspects include:

1. Reduction in net sales and, in turn, reduction in gross margin and profit

2. Creation of promotional image, based on consumer's expectations

In planning markdowns for the six-month plan, the buyer reviews last year's markdowns in dollars and as a percentage of actual sales.

The first step in planning markdowns is to establish an overall markdown percentage. This percentage is then multiplied by the total sales for the six-month period.

The next step is to distribute markdowns by month. To establish a percentage for each month of your six-month plan, use last year's markdown percent to sales figures (Figures 3.1, 3.3 and Perry's website) as a guide. The monthly percentage multiplied by the monthly planned sales establishes the monthly planned markdowns.

Because monthly percentages to sales figures do not total 100 percent, buyers often distribute markdowns using the percentage-by-month formula. This formula establishes season total markdowns as 100 percent, and each month is a percentage of that total. Refer to last year's markdown figures by month in Figures 3.1, 3.3, and on Perry's website.

The nature of the merchandise dictates the percentage of markdown, as does the time of the year. For example, the Christmas season is a strong regular-price selling season for lingerie and would dictate a later and less significant markdown than Christmas apparel and other seasonal goods. Most buyers would like to move their stock out of the store at the height of the season while customer traffic is heaviest. This can be accomplished with earlier and deeper markdowns.

Your next step is to review last year's markdowns, in both dollars and percentages, and industry averages. Last year's markdown figures by month can be found in Figures 3.1, 3.3, and on Perry's website. Industry figures can be researched in trade publications or by calling industry buyers. These will be your basis for establishing your departmental markdowns in both dollars and percentages.

SIMULATION
Go to Figure 3.7 in the book or on Perry's website.

The Figure 3.7 worksheet in the book and on Perry's website will help you complete the next step of your six-month plan. Remember to first establish your percentage of markdown for each month of your plan.

Follow these steps:

1. Fill in plan sales by month and total.

2. Fill in total markdown dollars in the total markdown dollar column based on your established markdown percentage plan.

3. Distribute markdown percentage by month using the figures listed in Table 3.1 below as a guideline.

TABLE 3.1

	FEBRUARY	MARCH	APRIL	MAY	JUNE	JULY	TOTAL
MD% to Sales	29.5	26.7	24.5	20.9	28.5	33.1	
MD% by Month	15.9	18.44	15.24	13.35	18.44	18.63	100.0

	AUGUST	SEPTEMBER	OCTOBER	NOVEMBER	DECEMBER	JANUARY	TOTAL
MD% to Sales	28.0	24.3	25.3	22.3	24.2	48.1	
MD% by Month	15.17	12.88	13.92	15.17	25.02	17.84	100.0

	AUGUST	SEPTEMBER	OCTOBER	NOVEMBER	DECEMBER	JANUARY	TOTAL
PL Sales							
MD % to Sales							
MD $							
MD % by Month							

Plan Sales × MD % to Sales = MD $

Justification of Plan Markdowns by Month:

August

September

October

November

December

January

FIGURE 3.7   Perry's worksheet for plan markdowns

PLANNING PURCHASES

The basic elements of your plan have been established in your worksheets. You have planned your sales, stock, and markdowns. When entered into the following formula, they establish the dollars (at retail) available to purchase merchandise.

> Planned sales
> + Planned EOM stock (the next month's BOM stock)
> + Planned markdowns
> − Planned BOM stock
> _____
> = Planned purchases at retail

The next step is to convert purchases into a cost figure. Before calculating cost, you must first plan your department **markup percentage**. Refer to the department cumulative markup percentage in Figure 3.3 and research current competitor's 10K financial reports on the Internet to see what other stores' markup percentage is for the same department. Once you determine your department markup percentage, enter the percentage on your six-month plan in the space designated at the bottom of the form. For plan purchases in the example below, the junior's cumulative markup percentage of 53.1% is used.

Planned purchases can be converted into a cost figure by multiplying the planned purchases times the markup complement (100 percent minus the markup percent).

EXAMPLE:

> Planned purchases = $100,000 (at retail)
> MU% = 53.1%
> $100,000 × (1 − 53.1%) =
> $100,000 × .46.9 = $46,900 planned purchases at cost

You are now ready to calculate your planned purchases. Use the worksheet in Figure 3.8 to complete your six-month plan.

Calculate all of your figures at retail and at cost.

Now you know the dollar amount available for market purchases at both retail and cost. When you work with a vendor to purchase merchandise, you will be given the cost of an item and must decide on the retail based on your department plan markup percentage. If an item costs $100 and your department markup percentage is 53.1%, the retail price would be determined by using the formula in the following example.

$$\text{Cost} \div (1 − \text{markup \%}) = \text{retail}$$
$$\$100 \div (1 − .531) =$$
$$\$100 \div .469 = \$213.22$$

SPRING	FEBRUARY	MARCH	APRIL	MAY	JUNE	JULY
FALL	AUGUST	SEPTEMBER	OCTOBER	NOVEMBER	DECEMBER	JANUARY
Plan Sales						
(plus) Plan EOM Stock						
(plus) Plan MD						
(minus) Plan BOM						
(equals) Plan Purchases at Retail						
(times) 100% – MU%						
(equals) Plan Purchases at Cost						

FIGURE 3.8 Perry's worksheet for plan purchases

$213.22 is not a typical retail price. The retail price could be rounded up to $214. To calculate the markup percentage with a retail of $214, use the following formula.

$$\text{Markup \%} = (\text{retail} - \text{cost}) \div \text{retail}$$
$$(\$214 - \$100) \div \$214 =$$
$$\$114 \div \$214 = 53.27\%$$

The **markup** is the dollar amount added to the cost of an item to determine the selling price of an item and cover expenses and profit. Using the example above, markup is calculated by the following formula.

$$\text{Markup} = \text{Retail} - \text{Cost}$$
$$\$214 - \$100 = \$114$$

Not all purchases are made using the exact department markup percentage. If an item has a higher perceived value, the retail price could be at a markup percentage higher than plan. There may also be items that a buyer would retail at a lower than plan markup percentage to meet a particular price point or for a special sale. The important factor is that the aggregate purchases meet or exceed the department plan markup percentage.

After you have completed your six-month plan, you can calculate your average stock and your stock turnover for this six-month period.

All of your information should be transferred to the blank six-month plan on Perry's website.

STUDIO:

SIMULATION
Go to Figure 3.8 in the book or Perry's website. The blank six-month plan can be found on Perry's website.

OPEN-TO-BUY

Open-to-buy (OTB) is the check-and-balance system built into the six-month plan. It allows the buyer to regulate or adjust inventory levels according to actual sales. It acts as an escape valve. If sales are down in relation to the plan, adjustments can be made to the purchases to prevent overstocking. If sales exceed the plan, additional merchandise can be purchased to prevent an understocked selling floor.

Open-to-buy is the number of dollars available to purchase merchandise that is not accounted for by previous purchase orders.

Planned purchases
– Outstanding purchase orders not yet delivered
_____
= Open-to-buy

To understand this concept, we must look at the entire formula:

Planned sales for August	$20,000
+ Planned EOM stock for August	$25,000
− Planned markdowns for August	$500
= Merchandise required	$45,500
− Planned BOM stock for August	$25,000
= Planned purchases for August	$20,500
− On order for August	$15,500
= Open-to-buy for August	$5,000

As we already know, the six-month plan is completed well in advance of (four to six months) the season. The buyer in the example spent or placed orders for all but $5,000 of available money. If in July there is a downward trend in sales, with actual sales below plan by $3,000, then the open-to-buy would decrease by the same amount.

Actual sales	$17,000
+ EOM stock	$25,000
+ Markdowns	$500
= Merchandise required	$42,500
− BOM stock	$25,000
= Purchases	$17,500
− On order	$15,500
= Open-to-buy	$2,000

This is the essence of inventory control. Available money is decreased to prevent overstocking. Remember, merchandise requirements are based on the relationship of stock to sales. This same system also works in a positive direction. If sales are beyond the buyer's projections, open-to-buy will increase proportionately.

STEP 4

Develop Assortment Plan

IN THIS CHAPTER, YOU WILL LEARN:

* To analyze merchandise needs by classification, subclassification, fabrication, color, size, price points, and units
* To rank merchandise needs by percentage and dollars

In this chapter, the new buyer develops an assortment plan, which involves several tasks, to include reviewing the department's classifications, considering subclassifications, taking into account aspects such as fabrication and color, determining sales by month, and calculating price points and price lines.

CLASSIFICATIONS

Department store buyers have the monumental task of budgeting large sums of money and determining how that money is to be spent. As do most wise financiers, these buyers begin with a plan. This plan converts large sums of money into *classifications* of merchandise to be carried in their departments. This breakdown of merchandise by classification (e.g., pants, shirts, sweaters, for apparel) is called an *assortment plan*.

An assortment plan ultimately allows the buyer to examine the department from the perspective of merchandise needs in relation to style, fabrication, color, size, and price lines.

Your first step in developing an assortment plan is to review the classifications that presently exist in your department. You will find the classifications and percentages of sales produced for last year's fall/holiday season in all seven departments on Perry's website.

Table 4.1 is an example for the juniors' department.

TABLE 4.1

JUNIORS' CLASSIFICATIONS FOR FALL/HOLIDAY		
CLASSIFICATION	PERCENT	SALES IN MILLIONS
Sweaters	15.0	$ 3,915,000
Tops	20.0	$ 5,220,000
Shirts/Blouses	6.0	$ 1,566,000
Jackets	5.0	$ 1,305,000
Pants	14.0	$ 3,654,000
Shorts	2.0	$ 522,000
Jeans	18.0	$ 4,698,000
Activewear	8.5	$ 2,218,500
Skirts	2.5	$ 652,500
Dresses	8.0	$ 2,088,000
Swim	1.0	$ 261,000
TOTAL	100.0	$26,100,000

You must decide if any additional classifications for new merchandise should be added or if dated classifications should be deleted. It is the buyer's job to continually update classifications to remain current with the marketplace. Sales by classification should be reviewed to see how the marketplace and the consumer might adjust the percentage that each classification produces. Review your research and look through trade magazines to refresh your memory.

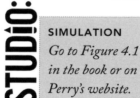

STUDIO:

SIMULATION
Go to Figure 4.1 in the book or on Perry's website.

List your department's classifications in Figure 4.1. Next, determine what percentage of sales each classification accounts for in the total fall/holiday plan. Your percentages should equal 100 percent. To complete Figure 4.1, these percentages can be multiplied by the total planned sales for the fall/holiday season.

MONTHLY SALES BY CLASSIFICATION

Now that you have determined your season sales by classification, you need to distribute them by month.

PERRY'S

SALES BY CLASSIFICATION, PERCENTAGE, AND DOLLARS

CLASSIFICATION	PERCENT	×	SEASON SALES	=	CLASS SALES
_____	_____		_____		_____
_____	_____		_____		_____
_____	_____		_____		_____
_____	_____		_____		_____
_____	_____		_____		_____
_____	_____		_____		_____
_____	_____		_____		_____
_____	_____		_____		_____
_____	_____		_____		_____
_____	_____		_____		_____
_____	_____		_____		_____
TOTAL	100%				_____

FIGURE 4.1 Perry's sales by classification, percentage, and dollars

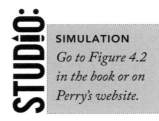

STUDIO:
SIMULATION
Go to Figure 4.2 in the book or on Perry's website.

Complete Figure 4.2 by following the steps detailed below. On Perry's website, Figure 4.2 is color-coded to help you understand what information is needed and where to transfer the information.

STEP 1 Using Figure 3.5 from the previous chapter, transfer the monthly sales distribution percentages to the top line of Figure 4.2. The sum of these percentages must equal 100 percent.

STEP 2 Using Figure 4.1, transfer all of the fall/holiday classifications (pants, shirts, etc.) into the designated spaces.

STEP 3 Using Figure 4.1, transfer the fall/holiday class sales into the last column.

STEP 4 Copy monthly sales from Figure 3.5 in the previous chapter, listing total sales in dollars by month across the bottom of the page. Total monthly sales should equal sales plan for the season.

STEP 5 Multiply the monthly sales percent by each classification sales figure to get the monthly sales by classification. (There are two versions of the Figure 4.2 electronic worksheet on Perry's website. One is without embedded formulas and one is with embedded formulas, so that figures will calculate automatically.)

EXAMPLE:

If the classification of tops will produce 20% of the six-month fall/holiday sales of $26.1 million, the total classification sales for the six-month period equates to $5,220,000 (.20 × $26,100,000).

If August sales are 14.9% of the fall/holiday six-month sales, then tops for August would be calculated as 14.9% × $5,220,000 = $777,780.

SUBCLASSIFICATIONS

Although the merchandise focus has narrowed, the dollar amounts by classification are still too large to provide accurate buying information. Your next step is to develop *subclassifications*. These subclassifications allow a buyer to be more precise in analyzing and forecasting the merchandise assortment. For example, a sweater classification could be further subdivided into crewneck, V-neck, tunic, and cardigan.

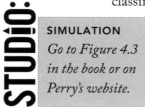

STUDIO:
SIMULATION
Go to Figure 4.3 in the book or on Perry's website.

In some departments, classifications are not further separated into subclassifications. This is not the situation for departments in which buying is more specialized.

Using the form in Figure 4.3, develop subclassifications for one classification in your department.

CLASSIFICATION SALES BY MONTH

	FEBRUARY AUGUST	MARCH SEPTEMBER	APRIL OCTOBER	MAY NOVEMBER	JUNE DECEMBER	JULY JANUARY	TOTAL
PERCENT	_____	_____	_____	_____	_____	_____	100%

CLASS   TOTAL SALES

_____	_____	_____	_____	_____	_____	_____	_____
_____	_____	_____	_____	_____	_____	_____	_____
_____	_____	_____	_____	_____	_____	_____	_____
_____	_____	_____	_____	_____	_____	_____	_____
_____	_____	_____	_____	_____	_____	_____	_____
_____	_____	_____	_____	_____	_____	_____	_____
_____	_____	_____	_____	_____	_____	_____	_____
_____	_____	_____	_____	_____	_____	_____	_____
_____	_____	_____	_____	_____	_____	_____	_____

TOTAL SALES   _____ _____ _____ _____ _____ _____

FIGURE 4.2 Perry's classification sales by month

CHAPTER 4 • STEP 4: DEVELOP ASSORTMENT PLAN // 57

PERRY'S

SUBCLASSIFICATIONS FOR _____ CLASSIFICATION

1. _____

2. _____

3. _____

4. _____

5. _____

6. _____

7. _____

8. _____

FIGURE 4.3 Perry's subclassifications

OTHER FACTORS IN ASSORTMENT PLANNING

Buyers analyze their merchandise needs by factors other than classifications and subclassifications. You should also consider fabrication, color, size, vendor, and price lines. Figure 4.4 shows an example of a plan by percentage for fabrication, color, size, and vendor for the juniors' top classification. Use this plan only as a guide; your research will help you make adjustments for your new assortment plan.

You are now ready to plan your classification by fabrication, size, and vendors. Fill in the information on Figures 4.5, 4.6, 4.7, and 4.8.

SIMULATION
Go to Figures 4.5, 4.6, 4.7, and 4.8 in the book or on Perry's website.

STUDiO:

PRICE LINES

The last step of the assortment plan is to determine how the buyer spends the budgeted dollars, both in units and by *price line*. Before completing this exercise, purchases should be distributed by classification.

To find the total purchases, refer to your completed six-month dollar plan. Total planned purchases equal the six-month sum of August through January planned purchases. Transfer your total dollar purchases to the bottom line of Figure 4.9. Transfer the classification percentages from Figure 4.1 to Figure 4.9. Now multiply the classification percentage by the total dollar purchases to arrive at the total purchases by classification. When you have completed Figure 4.9, you will have a more accurate picture of the dollars available to spend by each classification.

SIMULATION
Go to Figures 4.1 and 4.9 in the book or on Perry's website.

STUDiO:

The final use of the assortment plan is to determine how the buyer spends the budgeted dollars both in units and by price line. This procedure is illustrated in the following example:

CLASS A	PRICE LINE		# OF UNITS	$ BY PRICE LINE
	$20	30%	_____	$ 300,000
	$25	50%	_____	$ 500,000
	$30	20%	_____	$ 200,000
TOTAL CLASS				$1,000,000

We know that 50 percent of the total sales was produced at a $25 price line; hence, $1,000,000 times 50 percent equals $500,000. This is how much you have to spend on the $25 price line. The same procedure is followed to determine the dollar purchases for the remaining price lines.

(Percentages based on total department sales)

FABRICATION:

Cotton	55%
Linen	5%
Spandex	20%
Polyester/Nylon	15%
Wool	5%
	100%

COLOR:

Solids	40%
Stripes	20%
Plaids	10%
Prints	30%
	100%

SIZE:

3	1	S	3
5	2	M	5
7	3	L	4
9	3		12
11	2		
13	1		
	12		

VENDOR FOR DENIM JEANS:

Lulu	8%
Roxy	5%
Paige	6%
Soprano	4%
Rag and Bone	8%
7 for All Mankind	10%
Jolt	7%
Fire	7%
Vigoss	9%
Articles of Society	6%
Other, including private label	30%
	100%

FIGURE 4.4 Perry's juniors' department assortment planning factors for last year

PERRY'S

ASSORTMENT PLAN BY FABRICATION
FOR ______________ CLASSIFICATION

FABRICATION DISTRIBUTION	PERCENT TO TOTAL
	100%

JUSTIFICATION:

FIGURE 4.5 Perry's assortment plan by fabrication

PERRY'S

ASSORTMENT PLAN BY COLOR

FOR _____ CLASSIFICATION

COLOR DISTRIBUTION | PERCENT TO TOTAL

_____ | _____

_____ | _____

_____ | _____

_____ | _____

_____ | _____

_____ | _____

_____ | _____

_____ | _____

100%

JUSTIFICATION:

FIGURE 4.6 Perry's assortment plan by color

PERRY'S

ASSORTMENT PLAN BY SIZE

FOR _____ CLASSIFICATION

SIZE DISTRIBUTION   PERCENT TO TOTAL

_____   _____

_____   _____

_____   _____

_____   _____

_____   _____

_____   _____

_____   _____

_____   _____

_____   _____

                                     100%

JUSTIFICATION:

FIGURE 4.7 Perry's assortment plan by size

PERRY'S

ASSORTMENT PLAN BY VENDOR
FOR ______________ CLASSIFICATION

VENDOR DISTRIBUTION	PERCENT TO TOTAL
	100%

JUSTIFICATION:

FIGURE 4.8 Perry's assortment plan by vendor

CLASSIFICATION	PERCENT	×	SEASON PURCHASES	=	CLASS PURCHASES
_____	_____		_____		_____
_____	_____		_____		_____
_____	_____		_____		_____
_____	_____		_____		_____
_____	_____		_____		_____
_____	_____		_____		_____
_____	_____		_____		_____
_____	_____		_____		_____
_____	_____		_____		_____
_____	_____		_____		_____
TOTAL	100%				_____

FIGURE 4.9 Perry's purchases by classification, percentage, and dollars

To determine the number of units you can purchase, divide the price line dollars by the price line amount.

EXAMPLE:

$$50\% \text{ of } \$1,000,000 = \frac{\$500,000}{\$25 \text{ Price Line}} = 20,000 \text{ units to be purchased}$$

Now the buyer knows approximately how many units at a $25 selling price will be needed to meet the six-month plan.

You should realize that a buyer's plans are comprehensive and help narrow the focus on the monumental task of spending large sums of money.

Complete Figure 4.10 using plan purchases by classification to detail each classification by price line, units, and season-dollar totals. You will have to duplicate this page according to the number of classifications you have planned.

STUDIO:

SIMULATION
Go to Figure 4.10 in the book or on Perry's website.

PERRY'S

ASSORTMENT PLAN BY PRICE LINE, UNITS, AND DOLLARS

CLASSIFICATION	PRICE LINE	# OF %	$ BY UNITS	CLASS PRICE LINE	TOTAL
_____	_____	_____	_____	_____	
	_____	_____	_____	_____	
	_____	_____	_____	_____	$ _____
_____	_____	_____	_____	_____	
	_____	_____	_____	_____	
	_____	_____	_____	_____	$ _____
_____	_____	_____	_____	_____	
	_____	_____	_____	_____	
	_____	_____	_____	_____	$ _____
_____	_____	_____	_____	_____	
	_____	_____	_____	_____	
	_____	_____	_____	_____	$ _____

FIGURE 4.10 Perry's assortment plan by price line, units, and dollars

## CHAPTER 5

STEP 5

How to Shop the Market

IN THIS CHAPTER, YOU WILL LEARN:

* How to prepare for your market trip
* What type of statistics and department information are needed before your trip to the market
* The different methods used to shop the market
* How to assess market trends for your department
* How to develop key resources
* The buyer's role in the market

A buyer travels to the *market* both to visit trade shows and to meet with individual vendors of merchandise that the buyer's store either carries or would like to consider carrying. The typical buyer of a small- to medium-size department store might travel to the market or visit vendors anywhere from five to nine times per year. Employees from boutiques, specialty stores, and large department stores might visit more often, and most stores would have the vendor's representative visit their corporate headquarters or the location where the buyer works. The frequency of the market trips is based not only on the size of the organization but also on the location and distance to the market, the department's target customer and his or her fashion innovation, and the structure and philosophy of the organization's management.

Depending on the location, the buyer may be in market for as little as one day or, if visiting foreign markets or overseas factories, the trip might extend beyond a week. The nature of the trip—whether it is to actually purchase merchandise, to seek out new trends and vendors, or to develop product overseas—dictates the amount of time in market. The cost of market trips is significant; buyers today have limited funds and, therefore, must live within their travel budget. The cost-benefit of a market trip must be evaluated against the goals of that trip, and buyers must maximize their efforts to improve the profitability of their department. This requires buyers to preplan their market visits to make sure each trip is productive.

PRE-MARKET PLANNING

Timing of market trips is generally based on predetermined market dates that are set by each industry. For example, a menswear buyer might go to one of many websites to determine which markets he or she would like to attend for each buying season. We Connect Fashion is a search engine for the fashion industry that provides market calendars based on apparel classifications, city, and month (http://weconnectfashion .com/). Each listing also designates whether a show is for menswear, women's wear, or children's wear and where it will be located. Further information on the website will also lead the buyer to the website of the trade show so that person can register and explore the organization of the show itself. Market websites traditionally inform the buyer of what classifications of merchandise will be shown, which vendors are renting booths at the show, and the actual floor plan of where the booths will be located (by number on a map). Additional information, such as seminars, fashion shows, and other events, may be listed, as well as registration information.

STUDIO:

SIMULATION

Using the We Connect Fashion website, find a series of pages that lead you to the **Men's Apparel Guild in California (MAGIC)** *Trade Show in Las Vegas or the ENK website that organizes numerous trade shows throughout the world. These websites (www.magiconline.com or www.enkshows.com) will take you to numerous tradeshow websites.*

Explore these sites and research the following information:

* *Date of the next market*
* *Show floor categories*
* *Show floor plans with booth numbers*
* *List of seminars, fashion shows, and events*

Present a report to your divisional merchandising manager (DMM) on the trade show that is most appropriate for your department and state the reasons why you should attend this market.

RESEARCH BUSINESS STATISTICS

Approximately two weeks before the buyer travels to the market to purchase merchandise, the buyer reviews the six-month dollar plan, the merchandise assortment plan, and the open-to-buy report, but he or she must also evaluate if the business goals from the previous season were met. The buyer should assess his or her performance by overall gross margin or maintained markup and also by classification and by vendor. This provides the buyer with information to review the performance of each vendor, to reassess each classification for viability and vitality, and to determine where growth and profitability for the department lies. The buyer will have a list of new vendors to visit, in addition to the performance of each major vendor in the department and a list of concerns to discuss with each vendor, including overall financial performance, shipping dates, order completion, order performance by styles or collections, and markdown money for those purchases that performed poorly. More information on negotiating many of these issues is discussed in Chapter 7.

Buying plans allow the buyer to examine present business conditions and project future performance for the department. A buyer reviews the plans to see how much money was spent for each period or month and how many units were purchased and delivered. With this information, the buyer projects forward to anticipate how much is on-hand (BOM stock) and how much should be ordered (planned purchases). To prepare for market, the buyer needs more specific information about what has sold and performed well and what merchandise has not met the profit goals for the department. Most department stores have numerous reports that support the research a buyer will need. Classification reports and unit sales reports will supply the buyer with information about trends by classification and by style. A vendor performance report will show profitability by each manufacturer. An open-to-buy report will let the buyer know of canceled orders, sales adjustments, actual markdowns, and other data that may affect what is available to spend in market. All of this data helps the buyer determine the strengths and weaknesses in last season's purchases and analyze the current selling trends that will move into the next season.

In addition to the statistical information, the buyer needs to review promotional plans, special events, and the promotional calendar for the upcoming season to ensure that the right promotional merchandise is available for each month or event at the right price and in the right amount to meet consumer demand. With this research in hand, the buyer is ready to make appointments with vendors and shop the market.

There are many different ways to shop the market, and planning the itinerary depends on which market you attend and what type of merchandise you plan to buy. For example, if a buyer is shopping the New York City fashion market, which is organized primarily by building addresses within a three- to four-block radius, the buyer might shop by location or building to save time and to be more efficient. But if the buyer is shopping an apparel mart in Atlanta, the buyer might decide to shop by classification. This allows the buyer to keep color stories intact, critically shop each resource, and to take more fluid buying notes.

Although this method requires more hours, a new buyer may find it helpful to think about only one classification at a time. For example, if the buyer is shopping for dresses for the juniors' department, the buyer might spend a Tuesday afternoon at the Atlanta market meeting with only *resources* that sell dresses. At the end of the day, the buyer will review the notes he or she took at each vendor appointment, as well as line lists or sketches. This narrowed vision might be less confusing and improve buying decisions compared to shopping many different classifications at the same time.

The third way to shop the market is to organize appointments by price points or price zones, such as budget, moderate, or designer. Apparel markets or buying organizations often group manufacturers by similar customer base. Designer merchandise may be located in specific buildings in New York City or on a specific area of the layout or floor plan at MAGIC at the Las Vegas Convention Center or the AmericasMart in Atlanta.

Regardless of which way the buyer decides to shop the market, he or she sets appointments with the most important resources (vendors) based on sales volume and sell-through of units. This guarantees that these vendors have reserved enough time for the meeting, and the vendor can be prepared to discuss the store's account, sales, and any other issues that both parties deem to be necessary. Appointments establish the buyer's priorities in market and ensure that each meeting will be productive. Buyers must also plan to seek out new resources, so time should be scheduled for shopping new resources and determining new trends. Buyers also shop the competition or other major retailers that are trendsetters or benchmarks for superior retailing. For example, a buyer who is attending fashion market week in New York City would shop all of the major department stores, visit select boutiques with a similar customer base, and observe people and their dress and lifestyle. That same buyer, if attending fashion week in Paris, would visit major department stores such as Galleries Lafayette and Le BonMarche and browse the boutiques of the trendy Marais district.

GETTING ORGANIZED

The buyer must organize a significant amount of information before going to market. First, he or she must bring the resource list with all of the pertinent contact information for each vendor. The buyer's file should include resource name, address, and phone number; manufacturer's representative's name, address, and phone number; and the names of each vendor's principals or executives. These should be organized both alphabetically and by showroom address. This helps the buyer be efficient while in the market.

For each resource the buyer plans to visit, there should be a dollar volume report, a list of problems or issues with that vendor, special notes about each vendor, and special requests or actions the buyer wants to ask of that vendor. During a typical appointment, the buyer and the vendor's *sales representative* might discuss the past season's sales, best sellers, worst sellers, future special promotions, markdown money to support lost margins, *vendor co-op* advertising dollars, and a review of the upcoming line or collection. A good buyer also understands that strong relationships with vendors are essential to success and might discuss more personal aspects of the sales representative's life, such as vacations, family, and hobbies before starting the business discussion of the meeting.

The buyer sets the tone of the meeting and must ensure that the agenda is at the forefront, not allowing the salesperson to dominate the meeting. This requires that the buyer be organized, articulate, and knowledgeable about the business with each vendor and what is needed from that vendor to be successful in the future. It is important that each buyer meet the principals of the company, who are often the ultimate decision makers. Developing a healthy rapport and sense of cooperation with the personnel of a company is essential; it is unprofessional to allow personal feelings for a manufacturer's salesperson to get in the way of doing business with that organization.

DISCOVERING TRENDS WHILE IN THE MARKET

There are many sources of trend information, and a buyer needs to be alert to the information that is spreading through the market. Listening to other buyers (even those from other stores) and manufacturer's sales representatives, as well as the fashion office and shopping the stores, will give the buyer many clues about what's hot in the fashion world. Each buyer must determine if the trend is right for the customer and if an item should be tested to see how the customer might respond. The buyer must decide how much should be purchased in order to make an impact and align with the fashion office direction, which stores should carry the merchandise, and how many open-to-buy dollars it would require. Remember that trends include not only styles but also color, fabrication, prints and patterns, and lifestyle items. The buyer must also be aware of the basic or classic merchandise needs of the consumer and plan for goods that sell season to season regardless of trends.

Experience will help a buyer determine the reliability of sources. Over time, a buyer discovers the most accurate and useful sources of information about the market and trends. Each buyer must make his or her own decisions and not be pressured into buying something that is not right for the customer. The buyer must also know what information should and should not be shared in the marketplace. For example, a buyer should never brag about special favors or deals granted by a vendor and should avoid talking about the store's problems or personality conflicts among the employees.

MARKET ASSESSMENT AND DECISION MAKING

At the end of each day in market, the buyer should review the notes from the many different appointments and what has been seen during that day. The buyer should sort information by classification, delivery dates, price points, and trend. This allows the buyer to eliminate those items that are not preferred or are a duplication of another, more desirable item. For example, if shopping for women's black pants, a buyer might see 15 different styles and fabrications, but must also keep in mind how many black pants actually are needed in that department. The buyer may decide on 5 styles and then pick the best of the 15 styles, filing away the information on the other 10 styles in case one of the first styles is unavailable.

The buyer determines desirability by determining if the merchandise is on trend, at the right price, the right quality, and available when needed. Apparel buyers must consider the right fit for their customer, and all buyers must consider the item's selling record if previously purchased. Manufacturers can entice the buyer by offering advertising money, exclusivity, markdown allowances or guaranteed gross margin, terms and shipping allowances, and/or off-price merchandise.

With all of this information in mind, as well as input from the fashion office, the buyer must eliminate merchandise from his or her want list in order to fit the open-to-buy. The buyer must then consider the sales floor and its physical appearance. How will he or she merchandise the purchases on the sales floor? Will the items hang together as a collection or be dispersed throughout the department? How many *t-stands* are in each department? *Rounders*? *Waterfalls*? A buyer also must think about the appearance of units in addition to dollars. When viewing a new seasonal line, the buyer often will ask for a *style out* with the manufacturer's sales representative; this is when the buyer places the merchandise under consideration on a separate sales display rack to determine how the selected merchandise would look on the sales floor.

Most department store buyers do not write an order—or what is commonly called *drop paper*—when they are actually viewing a line of merchandise. They usually review their appointments, including their notes and line sheets, and then determine what they plan to buy after returning to their home office, where they write their purchase orders on the store's standard purchase order form. Usually, their boss, the DMM, must approve all of the orders.

It is important for the buyer to be prepared for this meeting with the DMM. The buyer should arrange the purchase orders progressively from most to least important and should be able to explain how the purchases fit with the dollar plan and the assortment plan. The buyer must conceptualize what he or she wants to accomplish with the purchase. For instance, is the buyer trying to introduce new, trendy merchandise or merely filling in the holes of the basic merchandise assortment? Does the department want to expand in a certain classification or expand private label merchandise? The buyer has to make a case for, or defend, purchases based on departmental goals. One way to do this is to recap all of the orders by trends, dollars, and classification. The buyer uses this information with the DMM and with store personnel to inform them of what has been purchased for their individual stores.

Divisional merchandise managers do not automatically approve all orders that a buyer presents. Because they are considering a bigger picture, the managers will ask many questions regarding assortment, gross margins, and the negotiation process to improve the buyer's business. If a DMM does not approve an order, then the buyer can return later and reintroduce the items if the department's business or the market has changed.

DEVELOPING KEY RESOURCES

It is the buyer's responsibility to develop key resources that will contribute to and improve the department's business goals. Key resources are those vendors that constitute the largest floor space in a department and provide the most incentives, such as higher margins, promotional opportunities, and increased profitability. These vendors or key resources make the buyer a "bigger fish" in a very competitive market. The success of the department then becomes more important to that vendor, which encourages a team mentality or partnership between the buyer and the vendor.

Key resources need to understand how they fit into the financial plans and goals of the buyer's department and what the buyer expects from the relationship. Some of the extras that a key resource might provide are exclusivity, shipping, advertising dollars, markdown allowances, guaranteed gross margin, off-price merchandise, and special promotions to coincide with major store sales or new store openings.

Upper management may create a **_vendor matrix_** of preferred vendors based on the line's compatibility with the retailers merchandise and gross margin goals. The vendor-retailer relationship is often based on a pricing advantage to the retailer, as well as vendor support such as markdown assistance or promotional dollars. In return, the retailer agrees to commit floor space and significant inventory levels to the vendor.

THE BUYER'S ROLE IN MARKET

The buyer represents the department and store at all times. This is especially important while in market. It is essential that he or she meet vendors on a regular basis, and if the buyer is new, he or she should meet all of the vendors and be receptive to any complaints or problems. A buyer wants to develop a reputation for being professional, responsive, and fair. Although the fashion industry is huge, the marketplace is relatively small when it comes to the reputations of its members. No buyer wants to be labeled as unprofessional or burn any bridges that might limit his or her career aspirations or advancement in the future.

It is also imperative that a buyer knows store policy with regard to accepting gifts or even a vendor buying a meal. News of impropriety spreads quickly in the marketplace, and accepting a gift may put the buyer's job in jeopardy. Buyers are expected to dress and act professionally while on market trips and should maintain a professional demeanor in all social situations.

SHOPPING INTERNATIONAL MARKETS

Today's buyer is much more attuned to the international fashion marketplace and often travels to global markets and trade shows to purchase unique merchandise or key brands for the store. The luxury market is particularly sensitive to iconic fashion brands from France and Italy because of their quality, uniqueness, heritage, and consumer demand. However, because of numerous trade agreements and laws, the buyer must be aware of import quotas, tariffs, and trade restrictions that may impact the importing of international merchandise.

The constraints that impact the purchase of global merchandise include delivery of merchandise in a timely manner, cost-effective shipping, and the actual cost determination of the merchandise. Because of the currency fluctuations, international shipping, duty and agent fees, buyers often ask for a *landed duty paid cost* (**LDP**) in U.S. dollars to more accurately plan their purchases and determine if the retail price of the merchandise is feasible for their customers.

Planning to attend a global trade show or market is very similar to attending a domestic show but with a few additional planning steps. The buyer must have a passport that is current for at least the next six months and must obtain a visa for the countries visited that may require this step. The trip often includes other buyers and the DMM and/or the GMM. Plans are made to travel together to reduce costs and to maximize the effectiveness of the buying trip.

Generally, a car service and translator or an import agent must be arranged to meet the buyers at the airport, taking them to their hotel and helping them maneuver a foreign city and marketplace. The hotel must be convenient to the tradeshow or fashion district of the city and offer business services such as Wi-Fi and fax machines to facilitate communication with the home office. The hotel is often used to meet with vendors, so a professional business space for meetings is desirable.

If a foreign agent is used, he or she would plan appointments with specific vendors and act as a consultant for the local marketplace. It is imperative to maximize your time in the market because of the expense and limited time frame; therefore, plans and appointments are made in advance. If an organization is large enough, it may have a buying office in a major fashion capital such as Paris or Milan.

Another major difference in planning an international market visit is the securing of a letter of credit guaranteeing that the purchaser will pay the seller for the merchandise. This letter is arranged with the purchaser's bank in advance of the trip and is presented at each purchasing transaction. This arrangement ensures that both parties will complete the transaction as agreed upon: The seller delivers the merchandise as agreed and the purchaser's bank releases the funds.

Major fashion capitals are often a source of new and exciting trends that a fashion buyer would like to be in tune with. Visiting trade shows and cities like Paris, Milan, and Tokyo offer the buyer insight into fashion runway trends, up-and-coming designers, and street styles that influence the fashion world. Buyers must observe all aspects of fashion and integrate this information into their buying plans. The We Connect Fashion website offers both domestic and international fashion weeks and trade show schedules (www.weconnectfashion.com/).

SIMULATION

Choose three new vendors you would like to visit on your next trip to market. Develop a profile of each vendor to present to your DMM, explaining why you would like to carry that specific line in your department. Compare that vendor with your customer profile.

The information in your new vendor report should include:

* *Company name and parent company (if applicable)*
* *Address of sales office and manufacturer's sales representatives*
* *Principals of company*
* *Markets where the company shows its merchandise*
* *Product line description, including classifications and price points*
* *Store(s) (A, B, or C) where this merchandise would be carried*
* *Whether competitors of Perry's carry this merchandise*
* *Whether this merchandise fills a void in Perry's assortment or is a replacement for another vendor's products*

## CHAPTER 6

STEP 6

Plan Market Purchases

IN THIS CHAPTER, YOU WILL LEARN:

* The steps to plan a market trip itinerary
* The major market weeks
* The merchandise selection process
* To write purchase orders and compare terms of the sale
* To understand the flow of merchandise to the sales floor

Market trips are planned by the buyer primarily to purchase merchandise for each season. Other reasons for visiting the market include finding new product lines, building vendor relationships, and negotiating with resources. Buyers generally plan the number of market trips to be taken according to market dates, store and customer needs, and proximity of the store's location to the market.

PREPLANNING

Before scheduling a market trip for the opening of a season, detailed plans must be finalized and approved by the divisional merchandise manager (DMM) and general merchandise manager (GMM). A six-month dollar plan should be completed and a stock assortment strategy developed. The stock assortment plan determines relevant classifications, subclassifications, price points, units, colors, sizes, and fabrication. Trade magazines for your industry, such as *Earnshaw's, Women's Wear Daily (WWD),* and *Home Furnishings News (HFN),* should be perused, because these publications contain pertinent information on current market trends.

Now that you have executed a six-month plan, concluded the stock assortment plan, and understand your responsibilities while at market, you are ready to schedule a market trip to either New York City or another market appropriate to your merchandise assortment.

Market trips generally last three to four days. Airline reservations are often coordinated by the DMM's secretary or company travel agent. A hotel room should be booked for this trip for two nights, allowing you three days in the market. All reservations should be secured as far in advance as possible, because vacancies fill up rapidly during major market weeks.

The next task is to prepare an itinerary. Figure 6.1 is an example of an itinerary prepared by a children's wear buyer to a domestic market.

As reviewed in Chapter 5, suggested ways to shop the market are by vendor importance, classification, building, or price line. Because many vendors offer more than one classification of merchandise, the market will be shopped by resource, in order of importance.

Using the itinerary form in Figure 6.2, begin to schedule your market week appointments, contacting key vendors first. Be sure to include the company name, building and room number or trade show booth number, telephone number, and sales representative's name on the itinerary. An itinerary will be left with the divisional secretary and distributed to the DMM, GMM, fashion director, and other buyers in your division who will be traveling with you.

Refer to the Perry's website for a resource list of key vendors for your department. You should add additional resources of your choice. Keep in mind that the DMM typically spends time viewing major lines with each buyer in the division. On occasion, the GMM also accompanies the DMM. Therefore, be sure to confer with the DMM to select appointments so you can view the lines together.

Time should also be allotted for visiting local stores to shop the competition to look for new vendors and merchandising ideas.

Major domestic markets for women's ready-to-wear in New York City are traditionally held in January, March, May, August, and October. Transitional and Fall I are shopped in March, followed by Fall II in May. Holiday goods are available in August, and spring merchandise is offered in October. Summer apparel is at the market in January. In February and August, most menswear buyers attend the Men's Apparel Guild in California (MAGIC) show or the Mrket show in Las Vegas. The Atlanta International Gift and Home Furnishings show is the primary home fashions market, with major shows each January and July. Market dates may shift as a result of calendar changes and unexpected events.

STUDIO:

SIMULATION
Go to Figure 6.2 in the book or Worksheet 18 on the Perry's website and to your department's catalog/line list and Industry Statistics on the website.

PERRY'S

TRAVEL ITINERARY

BUYER   K. Videtic

DEPT.   Children's

HOTEL   Hilton Garden Inn/63 W. 35th St.

PHONE   212-594-3310

	MONDAY	TUESDAY	WEDNESDAY	THURSDAY	FRIDAY
8:00					
8:30		7 For all Mankind-Deb	Chloe - Jess		
9:00		80 W. 40th St	180 Madison Ave.	Stella McCartney-Sue	
9:30		212-764-3745	212-957-1100	210 11th Ave.	
10:00	Armani Jr.-Beth	Hudson- Susan	Versace - Cathy	212-627-1408	
10:30	717 5th Ave.	231 W. 39th St./401	200 Madison Ave		
11:00	212-209-3500	212-736-6260	212-753-9008		
11:30	Ralph Lauren-Kelly	Milly Minis-April			
12:00	650 Madison Ave.	231 W. 39th St.	Susanne Lively-Teri		
12:30	212-318-7000	212-827-0010	1410 Broadway/1502		
1:00			212-555-1212		
1:30		Lilly Pulitzer-Kate			
2:00	Little Marc Jacobs-Amy	550 7th Ave./21st Fl	Tartine et Chocolat - Pat		
2:30	1 Rockefeller Plaza	610-878-5445	131 W. 33rd St/1006		
3:00	212-965-4046	Un Deux Trois-Carrie	Zoe - Carolyn		
3:30	Burberry- Jill	530 7th Ave.	134 W.33rd St/1224		
4:00	1350 6th Ave.	212-695-1955	212-564-5100		
4:30	212-707-6745		Hartstrings-Claire		
5:00			100 33rd St/1141		
5:30			212-868-0950		

FIGURE 6.1 Sample Perry's travel itinerary

PERRY'S

TRAVEL ITINERARY

BUYER ____________

DEPT. ____________

HOTEL ____________

PHONE ____________

	MONDAY	TUESDAY	WEDNESDAY	THURSDAY	FRIDAY
8:00					
8:30					
9:00					
9:30					
10:00					
10:30					
11:00					
11:30					
12:00					
12:30					
1:00					
1:30					
2:00					
2:30					
3:00					
3:30					
4:00					
4:30					
5:00					
5:30					

FIGURE 6.2 Perry's travel itinerary

From your fashion office representative, you will receive a market-planning guide that recaps important topics covered during the market meeting (discussed in Chapter 2). Remember to review this planning guide again, because it contains an overview of the market, fashion direction in color, fabrication, and styling, along with a suggested resource structure for the entire store. Schedule a separate appointment to meet with your fashion office representative to discuss your department's merchandise needs as it relates to his or her directive. After conversing with the fashion office representative, you are ready to shop the market. You can find an example of a fashion office directive on the Perry's website.

OPEN-TO-BUY

In Chapter 3, open-to-buy was introduced as a part of the six-month plan. Buyers generally receive an open-to-buy report before their trip to market. Adjustments are made to the plan based on any orders that may have been canceled by either the buyer or the vendor. Other adjustments, such as return to vendor, increases or decreases in sales or markdowns, or any transaction that would impact the amount the buyer has to spend in market, are used to update the buyers' spending plans. This information is made available in an open-to-buy (OTB) report. An example of Perry's OTB monthly report can be viewed in Figure 6.3.

VISITING RESOURCES

When buyers begin shopping a line, vendors often provide catalogs with pictures or line lists to facilitate the selection process. Each item is given a style number that indicates to the manufacturer the particular season, silhouette, and fabric.

Merchandise is shown either by groupings or by items. While examining the merchandise, it is important to consider the price, styling, color, fabrication, and quality. First, determine what retail price will sell the merchandise, and then compare that to the actual cost. If the markup achieved is acceptable, then the item is worth the cost. Second, select styles reflective of customers' needs rather than your personal taste. It is of utmost importance to remember that the customers ultimately purchase the merchandise.

To make the selection process easier, eliminate the styles that do not meet your requirements. From the remaining selection, rank the styles in order of preference.

Open-to-Buy Report   (CGMRTO) PAGE: 58   09:50 AM

CO P1, MD A, RD 4, DG 026 SUITS

THIS WEEK (JUN:3/5) #24		Last Month (MAY)	Current Month (JUN)	JUN.:1/5 #22	JUN.:2/5 #23	JUN.:3/5 #24	JUN.:4/5 #25	JUN.:5/5 #26	JUL.:1/4 #27	CURR. MO. (MTD)	Next Month (JUL)	2 Nxt Month (AUG)	3 Nxt Month (SEP)
$ NET SALES	LAST YEAR	10,000	5,000	950	1,000	1,000	1,050	1,000	0	1,950	0	8,000	20,000
	PLAN												
	ACTUAL	3,801	0	558	0	0	0	0	0	558	0	0	0
	% PLAN:LY												
	% ACT.:LY												
	% ACT.:PLAN	(62)		(41)	(100)					(71)			
$ STOCK/SALES	P.O.S.												
	HOME OFF.												
	TOTAL												
$ MARK-DOWNS	LAST YEAR	0	0	0	0	0	0	0	0	0	0	0	0
	PLAN	2,000	5,000	950	1,000	1,000	1,050	1,000	0	1,950	0	0	1,000
	ACTUAL	0	0	0	0	0	0	0	0	0	0	0	0
$ STOCK/SALES	LAST YEAR	0.0		0.0	0.0	0.0	0.0	0.0	0.0	0.0			
	ACTUAL	9.4	0.0	9.2	0.0	0.0	0.0	0.0	0.0	0.0			
MARK-DOWNS/ SALES	LAST YEAR	0	0	0	0	0	0	0	0	0	0	0	0
	% PLAN	20	100	100	100	100	100	100	100	100	0	0	0
	% ACTUAL	0		0	0	0	0	0	0	0	0	0	5
# NET SALES	LAST YEAR	0	0	0	0	0	0	0	0	0	0	0	0
	PLAN	0	0	0	0	0	0	0	0	0			
	ACTUAL	0	0	0	0	0	0	0	0	0			
# AVERAGE STOCK	LAST YEAR	0.00	0.00	0.00	0.00	0.00	0.00	0.00	0.00	0.00			
	PLAN												
	ACTUAL	58.55	57.05	57.05	57.07	0.00	0.00	0.00	0.00	0.00			
# AVERAGE SALE	LAST YEAR	0.00	0.00	0.00	0.00	0.00	0.00	0.00	0.00	0.00			
	PLAN												
	ACTUAL	55.90	0.00	55.80	0.00	0.00	0.00	0.00	0.00	55.80			
# STOCK/SALES	LAST YEAR	68		10	0	0	0	0	0	10			
	ACTUAL		0.00	0.0	0.0	0.0	0.0	0.0	0.0				
# NET SALES	LAST YEAR	0	0	0	0	0	0	0	0	0	0	0	0
	PLAN	0	0	0	0	0	0	0	0	0			
	ACTUAL	0	0	0	0	0	0	0	0	0			
$ RECEIVED NOT SHIPPED	ACTUAL	2,568	0	0	0	0	0	0	0	0			
$ SHIPMENTS	PLAN	22,000	10,000	0	0	0	0	0	0	0	0	15,000	30,000
	ACTUAL	6,558	5,249	5,249	4,680	0	0	0	0	0			
MARK UP	% LAST YEAR	0	0	0	0	0	0	0	0	0	0	0	0
	% PLAN	32	32	0	0	0	0	0	0	32	0	35	35
	% ACTUAL	35	32	0	0	0	0	0	0	0	0	35	35
# RECEIVED NOT SHIPPED		48	0	0	0	0	0		0				
# SHIPMENTS													

	CURR. MO. (MTD)	Next Month (JUL)	2 Nxt Month (AUG)	3 Nxt Month (SEP)
# OPEN-TO-RECEIVE	0	0	0	0
# ON ORDER	0	0	0	0
# OPEN-TO-BUY	0	0	15,000	30,000
$ OPEN-TO-RECEIVE	0	15,000	23,160	16,400
$ ON ORDER	0	0	0	0
% MARK UP	0	0	35	35
$ OPEN TO BUY	15,000	15,000	23,160	16,400
$ CUM. OPEN-TO-BUY	15,000	15,000	38,160	54,560

FIGURE 6.3   Perry's open-to-buy monthly report

Buyers use various systems of ranking, such as 1, 2, 3, or single, double, and triple asterisks, or checkmarks. Select a system that works well for you.

The vendor's sales representative can also provide guidance in decision making by noting top-booking numbers or projected bestsellers. Many resources utilize road representatives who can indicate even better the most appropriate styles for a particular territory.

Once the initial numbers have been chosen, ask the vendor to do a style out by placing together all numbers selected. Make final eliminations if any duplication or overlap exists. It is much easier to narrow the line while you are in the showroom than to wait until later, when it is more difficult to remember styling details.

The final step is to negotiate prices and terms with the vendor and to discuss previous vendor performance. Terms of the sale are discussed later in this chapter as a separate topic; negotiation skills and vendor analysis are reviewed in Chapter 7.

WRITING PURCHASE ORDERS

Before writing purchase orders, you should review and analyze the lines at the end of the market trip to recheck for duplication and to determine the resources that are most advantageous to fill the store's needs. For this reason, it is not advisable to leave orders or drop paper while shopping the market—wait until returning to the store to finalize orders.

Some vendors request **bulk estimates** of quantities while the buyer is in the market. If you comply with this request, emphasize that a bulk estimate is *not* a confirmed quantity.

After careful selection of styles, a breakdown or distribution of quantities by vendor, color, size, and store should be allocated on a worksheet. The order worksheets should be totaled by cost and retail to determine the markup, as well as to compare plan dollars and units to the previous year's figures. When you are satisfied with the order, transfer the information to an order form. Most larger stores now transmit orders via **electronic data interchange (EDI)**.

Most stores use their own order forms for uniformity. A sample order form (purchase order) from Perry's Department Store is shown in Figure 6.4 and on the Perry's website. The retail store usually lists the conditions of the purchase on the back of the order form. Stores that do not have their own order forms use order forms provided by the vendor.

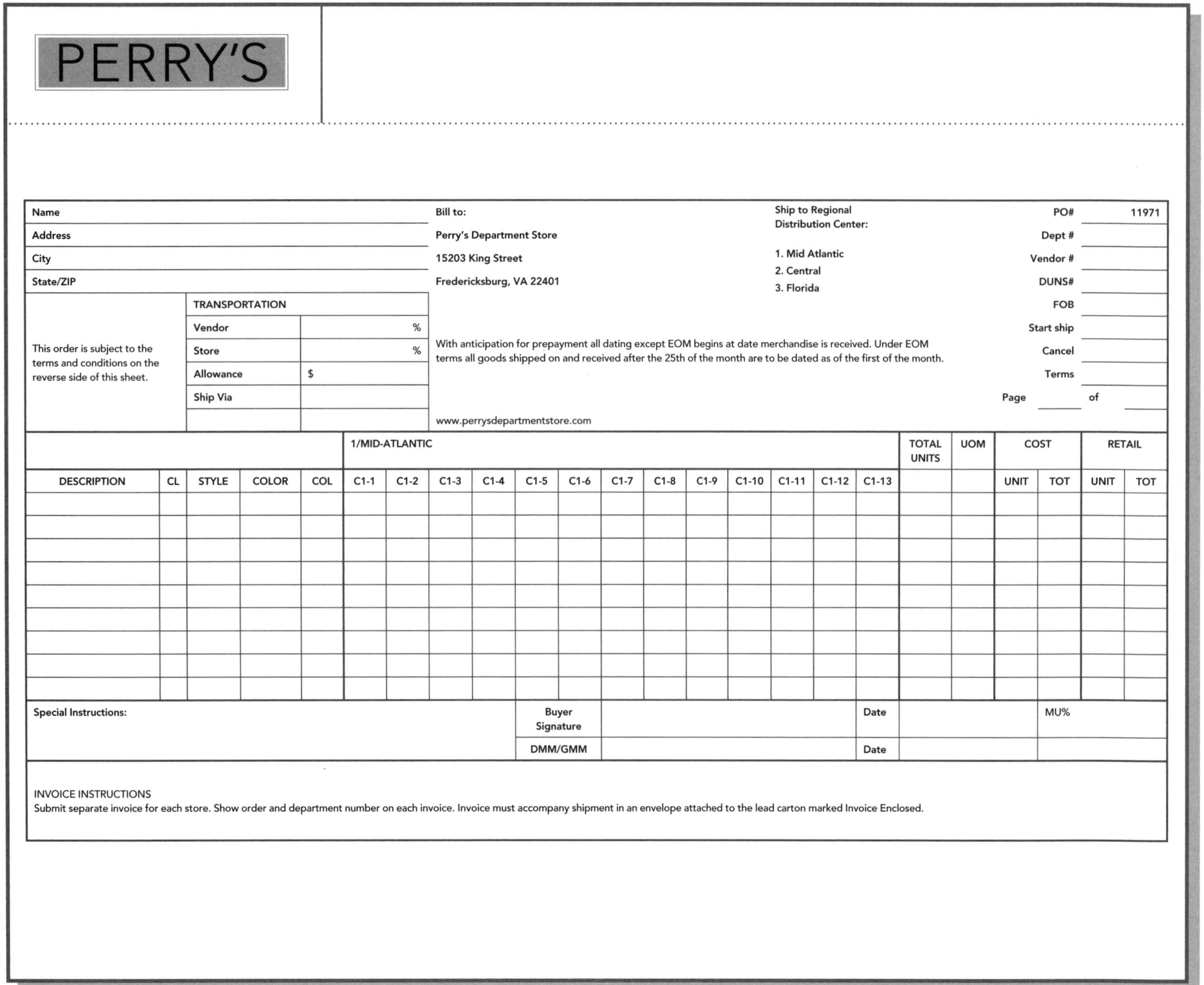

PERRY'S

Name
Address
City
State/ZIP

Bill to:
Perry's Department Store
15203 King Street
Fredericksburg, VA 22401

Ship to Regional Distribution Center:
1. Mid Atlantic
2. Central
3. Florida

PO# 11971
Dept #
Vendor #
DUNS#
FOB
Start ship
Cancel
Terms
Page of

This order is subject to the terms and conditions on the reverse side of this sheet.

TRANSPORTATION	
Vendor	%
Store	%
Allowance	$
Ship Via	

With anticipation for prepayment all dating except EOM begins at date merchandise is received. Under EOM terms all goods shipped on and received after the 25th of the month are to be dated as of the first of the month.

www.perrysdepartmentstore.com

					1/MID-ATLANTIC													TOTAL UNITS	UOM	COST		RETAIL	
DESCRIPTION	CL	STYLE	COLOR	COL	C1-1	C1-2	C1-3	C1-4	C1-5	C1-6	C1-7	C1-8	C1-9	C1-10	C1-11	C1-12	C1-13			UNIT	TOT	UNIT	TOT

Special Instructions:	Buyer Signature		Date		MU%
	DMM/GMM		Date		

INVOICE INSTRUCTIONS
Submit separate invoice for each store. Show order and department number on each invoice. Invoice must accompany shipment in an envelope attached to the lead carton marked Invoice Enclosed.

Figure 6.4 Perry's purchase order form

It is important to fill in all information accurately and legibly so mistakes will not be made in calculating and filling the order. At Perry's, a prenumbered order form consists of four copies. One copy is distributed to the vendor, another to the store's accounts payable department, another to the store's warehouse, and another to the buyer. Typical information needed to complete the order form is as follows:

* Date of order
* Department number
* Assortment rank and cluster
* Vendor name and address
* Vendor number (assigned by the store)
* FOB point
* Shipping instructions/routing
* Terms of sale
* Delivery/cancel dates
* Style number
* Classification number
* Description of merchandise
* Colors
* Sizes
* Quantity ordered
* Unit cost
* Total cost dollars
* Unit retail
* Total retail dollars
* Markup percent
* Buyer/DMM/GMM signatures
* Special instructions

Using the vendor catalog or line list found on the website for your department, select styles and write one order using the order form found on the website or in Figure 6.3. Be sure to review styles to eliminate duplication. For apparel, spend from $50,000 to $60,000 at retail for one delivery period for the mid-Atlantic cluster of stores. For home furnishings, spend from $12,000 to $14,000 at retail for one delivery period. Distribute merchandise to all stores within this store cluster and the appropriate store ranking. Be sure to research the market or apparel mart to plan for the correct week and to make sure that your key vendors are attending the show you plan to attend.

SIMULATION
Go to Figure 6.4 in the book or Worksheet 19 on the website and to your department's catalog/line list on the website.

When planning for delivery of merchandise, vendors will quote a delivery date consisting of a start ship date and a cancellation date. To further clarify the cancellation date, the store designates whether the merchandise is to be "shipped by" or "in store" by the cancellation date. For example, 8/1–8/25 "shipped by" cancellation means that goods can be shipped to the store beginning August 1, but can be shipped no later than August 25. Perry's uses a cancellation date that states "shipped by."

When the buyer purchases goods from the vendor, the means of transportation to the store must be decided. The transportation cost is part of the cost of the merchandise, and therefore careful consideration should be given to the means of delivery. Delivery terms will determine at what point ownership of the merchandise passes from the vendor to the store.

TERMS OF THE SALE

Because the buyer purchases inventory to sell at a profit for the company, the vendor's *terms of the sale* must be examined closely. The terms of the sale encompass discounts on the quoted price of merchandise, the timing of the payment, and the guidelines for transportation.

Vendors allow certain types of discounts to be taken on merchandise offered for sale. These reductions should be negotiated before confirming an order. Types of discounts include quantity discounts, seasonal discounts, trade discounts, and cash discounts. Discounts lower the cost of the goods, which, in turn, causes gross margin to increase.

Quantity discounts are extended to a buyer for ordering a large sum of merchandise. The discount is quoted as a percentage off the purchase price. For example, an item that sells at a line price of $20 might be reduced to $15, a 25 percent discount, if at least 600 units are ordered.

Seasonal discounts are offered on merchandise bought before the normal buying season. For example, if orders are placed for outerwear jackets 12 months in advance of the selling season, a reduced percentage (perhaps 15 percent) may be given by the vendor. This may also be called *incentive purchasing*.

Trade discounts are a percentage or percentages deducted from the retail list price of merchandise. An example is sterling silver flatware. The vendor establishes the suggested retail price and offers the buyer a trade discount off the list price. If the list price of a sterling silver baby spoon is $95, and the buyer is given a trade discount of 50 percent, the cost of the spoon would be $47.50.

Cash discounts are a percentage of deduction taken for paying an invoice within the specified time allowed. The discount motivates the purchaser to pay invoices on time. A common example of apparel terms is 2/10 EOM. If the invoice is paid within 10 days after the end of the month, a 2 percent discount may be deducted from the bill. If the payment is not made by the designated time allowed, the full amount of the invoice must be remitted with no discount deduction.

The amount of time allowed for payment of an invoice is referred to as **_dating_**. Types of dating include regular dating, EOM dating, extra dating, and receipt of goods (ROG) dating.

In **_regular dating_**, the cash discount and net periods are figured from the date of the invoice. An invoice date of September 5 and terms of 8 percent–10 days, net 30, would allow an 8 percent discount if payment is made by September 15. If the payment is made 11 to 30 days from the date of invoice, then no discount is allowed and the full, or net, amount is due. Payment made after 30 days is considered past due.

EOM dating is computed from the end of the month. Using 8/10 EOM as an example, an invoice dated October 10, with payment made by November 10, would receive an 8 percent discount. An exception to this is an invoice dated on or after the 25th of the month. These invoices are handled as if the invoice date was the beginning of the following month. Therefore, an invoice dated November 25, with EOM terms, would be due by January 10 in order to receive the 8 percent discount. Although not specified in the terms, it is understood that there is a 30-day net payment period from the end of the month before considering the invoice past due. Using the preceding example, an invoice dated November 25, with 8/10 EOM terms, paid on January 30, would not be past due, but the 8 percent discount would no longer be allowed.

Extra dating may be negotiated to allow a longer period of time to pay the invoice and still receive a discount. Extra dating is often requested for seasonal goods delivered early or for new store openings. For example, 2/10 + 30 indicates that an extra 30 days are permitted before payment, along with a 2 percent discount. Extra dating is typically listed in 30-day increments, such as 30, 60, 90 days, or beyond.

Receipt of goods (ROG) dating stands for dating based on the day merchandise is received. Rather than calculating the discount period from the date of invoice, the date the merchandise is delivered to the store is used to determine the payment period. ROG dating is used when the delivery period may be longer than usual because of a greater distance between the vendor and retailer. With ROG dating, the retailer avoids paying for merchandise before it has been delivered to the store and placed on the selling floor.

TRANSPORTATION

The retailer absorbs a major portion of the transportation cost. Therefore, the buyer must carefully plan the routing of goods from the FOB point.

The **FOB point** is the location where the merchandise changes ownership from manufacturer to store. FOB stands for free on board. The most widely used term is **FOB factory**, which means that the store takes ownership of the merchandise once the goods leave the factory of the manufacturer. In other words, the store is responsible for all of the freight charges plus insurance. **FOB store** means that the manufacturer pays all freight charges and insurance; this is a cost savings to the store. The buyer designates the shipper to be used for transportation. United Parcel Service (UPS) is often used for shipments of less than 50 pounds. Trucking companies are a cost-effective means of transportation, with a delivery time of three to five days, depending on the distance to the store. Air freight is the most expensive method of transportation, but it is often used when shipping merchandise from coast to coast or for deliveries needed in one or two days. The buyer must consider both the expense of transportation and the time frame for delivery.

Perry's has three distribution centers—one for each cluster located centrally in the geographic area. All merchandise is shipped to the designated cluster distribution center and then distributed to the individual stores. Purchase orders reflect which assortment each store should receive based on its ranking and its cluster. For example, the Tysons Galleria store in McLean, Virginia is ranked as an A store in the mid-Atlantic region and will receive the same merchandise assortment as the other A stores in the same cluster. Therefore, when you write a purchase order for an item, you must determine if it will go only to all A stores or to A and B stores or to all stores in that cluster or region. It is possible that it could go to all stores and to all clusters.

Also remember that this information is primarily about domestic markets and purchases. Imported merchandise requires other considerations that are discussed in Chapter 5.

BUYING CALENDAR AND MERCHANDISE FLOW

A buying calendar for apparel is provided in Chapter 2, Figure 2.1, to illustrate how seasonal purchases and delivery dates are designated by market.

Use this buying calendar as a guideline when planning purchases, and update it for any changes or shifts in market dates. A reserve fund of 5 to 10 percent of open-to-buy should be kept for immediate purchases of hot items, reorders, and off-price merchandise.

In some industries, certain basic styles are in constant demand by the consumer. Like many other stores, Perry's implements an automatic reorder system to maintain a "never out" stock status on staple items. Best-selling styles continue to reorder, changing fabrication by season. Fashion items, depending on the individual item, are on a 6- to 12-week cycle before markdown.

## CHAPTER 7

STEP 7

Negotiate Profitability

IN THIS CHAPTER, YOU WILL LEARN:

* The fundamental steps of effective negotiation
* How to recognize different styles of negotiation
* Several points to assist in negotiating in retail buying
* The importance of cross-cultural negotiation

Negotiation is part of our daily lives. We use it when we want to persuade someone to do something or to obtain something for ourselves. We negotiate with our families, our friends, our coworkers, and just about everyone we come in contact with. In order to be effective negotiators, it is important for buyers to first learn the fundamentals of negotiation.

NEGOTIATION PREPARATION

The most important part of the negotiation process is preparation. The first step in negotiating is to gather all relevant information and analyze the situation. For a retail buyer, this means you must learn as much as possible about the vendor's perspective (imagine yourself as the vendor's sales representative in order to gain that person's insight) and identify the related business issues, as well as your own departmental issues. Some of the information you might collect would include an assessment or evaluation of the vendor's performance for your department, the markdowns in dollars of that specific merchandise, or the percentage of your total dollar purchases from that merchandise.

With these facts, you could determine who has the advantage: the buyer or the vendor. For example, if a buyer is considering a purchase from a vendor, does the vendor need the buyer's business? Or does the vendor have highly desired merchandise that the buyer needs? In the first situation, if the vendor needs the buyer's business, then the buyer has the advantage. On the other hand, if the vendor has a brand name of merchandise that is in great demand by the buyer, then the vendor has the advantage. Having the advantage means more negotiating power, and negotiating power improves the possibility of getting a desired outcome. For a retail buyer, that desired outcome would mean a better price or improved profitability.

RELATIONSHIP POWER

If the buyer has a strong relationship with a vendor, then the power to negotiate is increased. A buyer who establishes rapport with a vendor will usually have a relationship style that is more cooperative than competitive. Buyers should see beyond the individual purchase and consider their affiliation with a vendor as a long-term association that creates prosperity and success for both retailer and manufacturer. The relationship between buyer and vendor should be considered a partnership that creates win-win opportunities.

As with any working friendship, there are many different ways to promote the relationship between buyer and vendor. Vendors remember birthdays and holidays, and buyers should do the same. Buyers can also improve their standing with a specific vendor by developing strategies that will increase sales for both. A buyer might develop special promotional plans with a specific vendor, such as in-store events like trunk shows or special giveaways, or purchase a selection of merchandise at a discounted price for a special event or sale.

Another method a buyer can use to create a stronger relationship with a vendor is to place significant orders. The higher the volume of purchases, the more important a buyer is to the vendor. A good buyer will build volume with fewer vendors to create relationship power. Remember that relationship power creates negotiating power.

As a part of the preparation, the buyer must consider the needs of the vendor to discover where there is room to negotiate. If the vendor has already given markdown money, there is less room to negotiate in other areas. The vendor usually grants markdown money based on a percentage of the retail purchases. The buyer should find out the vendor's expectations and anticipate possible objections. When working with the vendor at the start of a season, the buyer should in turn express company expectations for the department's purchases and profitability. After reviewing vendor performance and previous business arrangements, the buyer determines the negotiations to accomplish and sets objectives to achieve that goal.

For example, does the buyer want a lower price or for the vendor to pay for shipping? A strong negotiating plan includes opening, middle, and closing strategies. Good negotiators are flexible. A good buyer develops alternative strategies to cover all angles after presenting the initial offer. The buyer asks for what is needed to achieve departmental financial goals, while also understanding that a few concessions may be necessary to complete the business negotiation. A fair business transaction is generally a compromise somewhere in the midrange of what both parties are seeking. The best scenario is to have a win-win outcome where both parties get what they want and are satisfied.

NEGOTIATION MEETING

After the buyer prepares for negotiation and develops a plan or an agenda, the next step is to meet with the vendor. Determine who the leader and decision makers are so time is not wasted negotiating with someone who is not in a position to make a decision. A vendor's salesperson is often unable to negotiate buying terms, and the company's sales manager or principal must be included in the discussion. For best results, negotiate in person rather than by phone or e-mail and, if possible, keep negotiations between just two people. When additional parties are involved, there will be more discussion and opinions to be heard, resulting in a greater length of time before decisions can be made.

As the buyer begins the meeting, the first step is to build the relationship with the vendor and set the tone of the meeting. It is important that the buyer remain in charge and not let the vendor take control of the situation. When the buyer takes control of the meeting, it is then an appropriate time to present the offer or the problem or information in a clear and concise manner. The buyer should go through the agenda, making sure to cover all points, stating each request and supporting each request with facts. The more information and supporting facts a buyer has, the more likely it is that he or she will achieve a positive result. Remember to quantify information for a more powerful negotiating position: A "15 percent decrease in sales" is a more powerful statement than "sales are down." If the buyer is negotiating to resolve a problem, and the vendor's initial response is not what is desired, solicit assistance from the vendor. The buyer should ask the vendor for suggestions to help arrive at a solution that is acceptable to both parties.

A buyer's meeting agenda might look like this:

1. Thank the vendor for that person's support over the last quarter.

2. Review top sellers and each item's sell-through.

3. Review poor sellers and each item's sell-through.

4. Discuss margin results for the past season and, if not according to departmental plan, ask for vendor support for markdown money or dollar support to help bring margins in line.

5. Discuss late shipments and broken assortments for March and April.

6. Ask for *returns to vendor (RTVs)* for broken assortments, and markdown dollars for lost revenue caused by late shipments and broken assortments.

7. Discuss next market purchases with regard to terms and as a percentage of department's total volume, proposing a plan for regular and promotional merchandise buys.

Negotiations can be cooperative or competitive. Cooperative negotiation is most likely to result in a win-win situation. The interests and needs of both sides must be met for the negotiation to be effective. A good negotiator knows it is important to listen to the other person's needs, allowing him or her to speak without interruption. The buyer should respond with questions for clarification and summarize what has been said to acknowledge that the vendor's needs have been heard. The buyer should be ready to offer an alternate choice or concession if the negotiation hits a snag. Planning ahead of time about how to address a negative response will give the buyer more negotiating power. A cooperative negotiator exercises patience, listens carefully, and is open to compromise. A competitive negotiator who plays tough and uses intimidation to achieve desired goals may succeed, but this approach only creates a win-lose situation. It is therefore better to use persuasion rather than intimidation.

CLOSING THE NEGOTIATIONS

While planning for the negotiation meeting, prepare a checklist of points to review at the end of the meeting so that nothing important is overlooked. Repeat back to the vendor what has been agreed upon and how it will take place, including the time frame and any other details pertinent to the agreement. Assess the appropriate amount of time needed to close the negotiation and reach an agreement. Rushing to complete the negotiation can be as ineffective as taking too long to conclude. Be sure to document the agreement in writing, and preferably have both parties sign and date the agreement.

A checklist or closing review for Perry's might look like this:

POINTS TO REVIEW

1. Discuss late shipments and broken assortments in March and April

2. Review percentage of total merchandise that is invested with vendor

3. Review sell-through on March/April shipments and lost revenues

4. Ask for return of broken assortments sent in March and April

5. Ask for discount of new merchandise to counter lost revenue

6. Discuss chargebacks for RTVs

NEGOTIATION OF PURCHASES

There are many opportunities for the retail buyer to use negotiation skills. A buyer begins a season with negotiating terms of sale for purchases and ends the season with negotiating profit margin based on sales performance. Terms of sale to negotiate include:

* Payment terms

* Freight charges

* Price and discounts

* Allowances (markdowns, advertising, fixtures, signage, etc.)

NEGOTIATION OF PAYMENT TERMS

When the buyer views merchandise from a vendor, the vendor informs the buyer of the general payment terms offered by the company. The terms, referred to as dating, define the amount of time allowed before paying the invoice. Buyers sometimes negotiate for extra dating, which is additional time past regular terms to pay the invoice. If a vendor is promoting a new product but the buyer is hesitant to purchase the item, then the buyer may ask for an additional 30 or 60 days' dating to try the product while delaying payment.

Vendors may also offer dating programs for placing orders early for seasonal goods. In the home fashion market, vendors introduce Christmas merchandise in January. Because buyers do not take delivery of items until July or later and may want to wait until closer to the time of need before placing an order, some vendors may offer dating as of December 1 for a limited time to entice buyers to place orders early. This means instead of net 30 terms, a buyer could have Christmas merchandise on the selling floor for almost the entire season before paying the invoice on December 1. The benefit to the vendor is that best-selling items are identified earlier, allowing time to adjust production to more accurately anticipate sales.

Another common request for extra dating is when a new store opens. When a department store opens another location, a buyer typically requests additional dating for orders placed for the new store. Obviously, merchandise for the new store must arrive early enough to allow sufficient time to set the selling floor before the store's grand opening. Because the merchandise will not be available for immediate sales when it is received, the additional time before paying the invoice helps the retailer's cash flow situation. See Chapter 5 for more information on types of dating.

NEGOTIATION OF FREIGHT CHARGES

The retail store is generally responsible for paying freight on all incoming shipments once they leave the factory. Orders with such terms are FOB factory. Sometimes buyers will request the freight to be paid by the vendor, or FOB store. This is a cost savings to the buyer, as freight charges can be significant. The further a vendor is located from the retail store, the higher the freight charges will be. A buyer from a store located in California will often ask for a freight cap if the vendor is shipping from the East Coast. In this case, an agreed-upon percentage of the net total of merchandise is the maximum the buyer will pay. For example, a buyer may request that freight charges not exceed 10 percent of the total net cost of the merchandise. If the freight charges actually total 15 percent, the vendor will absorb the remaining 5 percent. If a vendor wants the order from the buyer, this may be a concession to do business with the buyer.

NEGOTIATION OF PRICE AND DISCOUNTS

A buyer can negotiate several types of discounts to reduce the quoted price of merchandise. Two of the most common are quantity and seasonal discounts. Buyers who place a high volume of orders may request a discount based on purchasing a large quantity of units. It is assumed that the greater the number of units ordered, the more cost-effective it is for the vendor to produce and ship the merchandise. A vendor often grants a discount, because the company would much rather make a sale of 3,000 units to one buyer than sales of 100 units to 30 buyers. The percentage of discount will vary depending on the volume of goods purchased.

A buyer may also negotiate a discount based on total dollar volume purchased from a vendor. For example, a buyer may promise the vendor a substantial increase of business over the previous year if the vendor will sell a specified amount of goods at 25 percent off on an order placed at the start of the season. Or, if the volume is high enough and the store is important enough to the vendor, the buyer may demand a certain percentage off all merchandise purchased.

Buyers also seek off-price opportunities from vendors. Merchandise that a vendor is closing out can be a product that has not sold well, odds and ends that are left over, or discontinued merchandise. **Closeouts** are offered at a discount that is greater than the usual percentage. There may be a limited quantity of each item, so vendors may prefer to sell an assortment of many different styles rather than allowing the buyer to select individual styles of merchandise. It is better to try to select merchandise in order to avoid purchasing unwanted styles that might not sell. Generally, assorted merchandise can be negotiated at a lower discount. Vendors may not offer off-price merchandise, leaving it up to the buyer to ask about what is available.

Seasonal discounts may apply for merchandise ordered in advance of a season. A vendor who sells Christmas merchandise may give a percentage off regular wholesale cost to all customers who make an early buy. In this case, to qualify, a predetermined minimum dollar amount must be purchased as early as January, but may not be shipped until July or August.

In the gift industry, vendors often give a case pack discount to all buyers who purchase in master pack increments rather than the minimum quantity. If an item sells at a wholesale price of $10 for a minimum of four units, then a vendor may offer a discount of 5 percent or more if the buyer will purchase the master pack of 24 units.

NEGOTIATION OF ALLOWANCES

Buyer negotiation for allowances is ongoing throughout the year. In the beginning of the year, new store, shortage, and advertising allowances may be negotiated in a contract, although some stores may negotiate advertising on a per-ad basis. Buying operations often ask for a new store percentage allowance in lieu of requesting merchandise discounts each time a new store is opened. The buyer may also request an allowance for shortage based on the percentage of department shrinkage.

Advertising allowance may be negotiated based on a percentage of net purchases from a vendor. If a vendor does not agree to provide an advertising allowance, then a buyer may load the cost of an item and, after the ad has run, charge the loaded amount back to the vendor as advertising allowance. This method is not favorable, because loading additional cost to the wholesale price of the item leads to an inflated and less competitive retail price.

Buyers should also discuss item substitutions, damages, merchandise exchange, guaranteed sales, and return policies with the vendor before ordering merchandise. It is best to note that no substitutions are to be made without approval from the buyer. Often a best-selling item may be sold out, and a vendor may request to substitute another style. The other style may be less desirable or may not coordinate with the collection purchased.

In a similar vein, if merchandise arrives damaged, most domestic vendors allow the buyer to return the merchandise. For imported merchandise, it is not cost-effective to return damaged or poor-quality items. In this situation, the buyer should negotiate a deduction from the full price. Some retail operations negotiate a percentage of net sales up front for damage allowance, but they charge a vendor back for any damaged merchandise that exceeds the allowance. If the merchandise is damaged, the retailer may charge the vendor the freight cost to return the goods. The vendor often accepts the chargeback for the damaged product, but requests that the retailer dispose of the goods rather than the vendor having to pay freight to return merchandise that is no longer of use.

The most important goal of a buyer is to make a profit for the company. Buyers analyze selling reports to determine the success and profitability of merchandise, comparing actual sales, markdowns, turnover, and gross margin to plan. When merchandise is not selling as well as expected, the buyer may either ask to return the product or request markdown assistance. Vendors are reluctant to accept returned merchandise for several reasons. Because the product has been opened and placed in the store for sale and marked with the retailer's tag, the merchandise may not be as saleable to another company. Also, it will be difficult for the vendor to find another buyer to take the merchandise after the season has begun. As a compromise, a buyer may ask to exchange the product for additional merchandise of a different type or reorder merchandise that is selling well. The buyer may also request a dollar allowance, or markdown money, from the vendor to share the markdown and salvage the profit margin. It is best to ask for assistance with markdown money as soon as poor-selling merchandise is identified.

A buyer has a better chance of receiving markdown assistance mid-season rather than waiting until the end of the season when most buyers review profitability.

For example, if the department plan for markdowns is 36 percent of net sales, and the vendor markdowns result in 40 percent of net sales, then the buyer would ask the vendor to help by paying the difference between 36 percent and 40 percent. If net sales for the vendor are $100,000, and markdowns total $40,000 or 40 percent, and the department plan allows for markdowns of 36 percent, or $36,000 on retail sales of $100,000, then the buyer would be over plan by $4,000. If the vendor purchase at cost has a retail markup of 54 percent, then the vendor share of the markdowns at cost would be $1,840.

$$\$4,000 \times (1 - .54) =$$
$$\$4,000 \times .46 = \$1,840$$

If a markdown allowance is granted, the vendor usually prefers that the buyer deduct the amount from the next invoice, rather than sending a check for the amount to the retailer. If the vendor invoice has already been paid, and a buyer is not continuing to do business with the vendor, then a debit balance will be created. The buyer will then need to try to persuade the vendor to write a check to the retailer, or will be forced to purchase additional merchandise to cover the amount of the debit. Sometimes a retailer will hold invoices from a new vendor in anticipation of any problems. Many buyers share selling reports with their vendors on a regular basis to prevent possible surprises at the end of the season.

Larger retail operations may negotiate a specific percentage of net sales up front to cover markdowns as part of an annual contract. Vendors are reluctant to accept this arrangement, but they often will agree in order to maintain business with a desirable account. Buyers may also discuss expectations of gross margin, negotiating a specified guaranteed margin agreement. Buyers at Perry's discuss poor-selling items with vendors when they are identified and discuss the vendor's overall sales on a quarterly and six-month basis.

For example, if purchases from a vendor total $500,000 at cost for a season, and the department plans a gross margin of 42 percent, then the buyer would need retail sales of $862,069 in order to achieve a gross margin of 42 percent.

$$\$500,000 \div (1 - .42) =$$
$$\$500,000 \div .58 = \$862,069$$
$$\$862,069 \text{ retail sales} - \$500,000 \text{ cost of goods} = \$362,069 \text{ gross margin dollars}$$

If the initial markup on the $500,000 purchase is 54 percent, then the retail of the purchase from the vendor would be $1,087,000.

$$\$500,000 \div (1 - .54) =$$
$$\$500,000 \div .46 = \$1,087,000$$

If actual sales for the season, after markdowns, total $840,000, then the profit dollars are $340,000, which is 40.48 percent and $22,069 short of the department plan at 42 percent.

$840,000 season retail sales − $500,000 cost of goods = $340,000 gross margin dollars, 40.48%
$340,000 actual gross margin dollars −
$362,069 plan gross margin dollars = −$22,069 (loss)

A buyer would ask the vendor to help pay for the loss of $22,069 gross margin dollars. Because the vendor purchases are at cost with a retail markup of 54%, the vendor cost would be $10,151.74.

$$\$22,069 \times (1 - .54) =$$
$$\$22,069 \times .46 = \$10,151.74$$

CANCELLATIONS

When a purchase order is written, signed, and submitted to the vendor, it is considered a binding contract. However, certain conditions may occur that lead a buyer to ask to cancel an order. When a department is overbought, management asks the buyer for ways to reduce the stock level. A buyer reviews selling history of merchandise and open orders to determine if any merchandise on order should be cancelled. If a classification of merchandise is overbought or not performing well, the buyer may seek to cancel additional merchandise on order for the weak classification to bring the **stock-to-sales ratio** in line. A reorder could be placed for an item that is not selling as well as projected. In cases such as these, the buyer should gather selling results to present to the vendor in support of canceling the merchandise.

Although facts support the cancellation, the vendor may have already produced the merchandise and may not be willing to let the buyer out of the contract. This is where negotiation skills and concessions come into play to create a win-win situation for both parties. The best scenario is that a buyer from another company needs that stock immediately and is willing to accept the order, but this is rarely the case. Perhaps the order can be moved to a future delivery date, giving the product a longer selling period to reduce stock. The buyer could always refuse the shipment when it is delivered, but this results in a win-lose situation that could strain the relationship. The buyer wins in reducing the stock, but the vendor loses when the merchandise is returned.

CROSS-CULTURAL NEGOTIATION

In today's global market, buyers must be prepared for cross-cultural negotiation. More buyers than ever are traveling widely to attend foreign trade shows and work with factories throughout Asia and other parts of the world, seeking a competitive advantage in pricing, uniqueness, or exclusivity. To negotiate effectively in the international business arena, it is crucial to understand the cultural differences and business etiquette of the country you desire to conduct business with. Business deals often fail because of the lack of understanding of values, beliefs, etiquette, and communication of a culture that differs from that of the negotiator. By accepting the fact that diverse cultures have different perspectives, the negotiator is less likely to view the situation in a negative manner.

Relevance of Time in Cross-Cultural Negotiation

There are distinct cultural differences when dealing with the perception of time. The two most commonly identified approaches to time management are known as monochronic and polychronic.

It is important to people from a ***monochronic culture*** to be punctual and to follow a schedule. Being late for a meeting would be considered disrespectful. Issues to be discussed are dealt with one at a time, in sequential order. This type of culture searches for facts to present specific information, with accurate details. Commitment is to the job, with less significance on relationships. Monochronic cultures include Germany, Scandinavia, Switzerland, the United States, and the United Kingdom. Negotiators in the United Kingdom sometimes use pressure strategies, including setting definitive deadlines. Decisions may take a longer time in Germany.

People from ***polychronic cultures*** are much more adaptable but are easily distracted. They are inclined to already have the facts. Polychronic negotiators are comfortable dealing with multiple situations and people concurrently. In Japan, a team of negotiators may come to a decision by consensus. Polychronic people are committed to long-term relationships. Schedules are flexible and punctuality is not important. Polychronic cultures take as long as needed to complete the negotiation, not allowing a schedule to dictate timing. This type of arrangement is more prevalent in Africa, France, Greece, Italy, and Mexico.

Personal Space

One aspect of personal space refers to the distance between people and whether they feel comfortable being touched. In China, Europe, Japan, and North America, many people like to have a space of two to four feet between themselves and the other party. They may also prefer not to be touched by those they do not know or feel comfortable with. But in Arab, Latin American, and Mediterranean cultures, people find touching acceptable.

Another consideration of space is associated with eye contact. In Arab and North American cultures, eye contact indicates truthfulness and reliability. Direct eye contact also conveys confidence. However, in other cultures, such as Japan, direct eye contact is considered rude and therefore avoided. Similarly, looking downward is a sign of respect in Asian cultures. When in negotiations with individuals from some Asian cultures, the preference in seating arrangements is to be side by side, whereas sitting across from one another is more favored in the United States.

Although many cultures today are incorporating a Western approach or a combination of both types of cultures, the buyer who makes the effort to learn about the culture of the vendor (or any business partner) will have a negotiation advantage over those who do not have this information.

## CHAPTER 8

STEP 8

Examine the Income Statement

IN THIS CHAPTER, YOU WILL LEARN:

* How an income statement relates to a buyer's performance
* How an income statement is used as a decision-making tool
* To calculate profit or loss using given information

Most individuals (employees and students in particular) view the concept of profit as the dollars generated by a business over and above operating expenses, which directly benefit the owners or upper management. Hence, they do not concern themselves with the income statement of their organizations. Why should they concern themselves with profits when profits have no bearing on them?

PROFIT OR LOSS?

As you progress into management, your focus will broaden to incorporate your store's income statement. This document provides you with a view of the company's financial health. It has become a pivotal decision-making tool and the mirror of the ultimate success or failure of you and your store. Buyers use the data to compare their departments' performance with other similar operations.

Gross margin, calculated before deducting operating expenses, is the indicator of your skills as a department store buyer. As a manager, attainment of the bottom-line profit or loss will necessitate decisions on your part. The income statement offers the big picture and is a necessary part of a retailer's education.

Profit (or loss) often influences management decisions and *does* have a direct bearing on employees' salaries. Management makes salary decisions based on dollar profits. Will all employees get a cost-of-living increase? Will those same employees receive merit raises? Profits or losses will probably play a major role in these and many more management decisions. Another example might be the assignment of square footage to a department based on its profitability. If a department increases its sales and profits, the departmental square footage will often be increased, too.

COMPONENTS OF THE INCOME STATEMENT

Figure 8.1 is an example of an abbreviated or simplified income or operating statement. As implied, this document presents information related to how much income is generated and how dollars are spent to operate a retail organization. Four elements constitute the profit mix: sales volume, cost of goods sold, operating expenses, and net other income.

Sales

Sales volume is determined by multiplying the unit retail price by the number of units sold.

EXAMPLE:

$$\$17 \text{ unit price} \times 100 \text{ units} = \$1,700$$

Gross sales are the total sales before any adjustments have been made in response to customer returns, customer allowances, and sales discounts.

Gross sales minus customer returns (credits or cash), customer allowances (reductions in the original price resulting from damaged merchandise), and sales discounts (employee discounts, preferred customers, etc.) equal net sales.

Gross sales	$50,000
– Customer returns, allowances, & discounts	$5,000
= Net sales	$45,000

Cost of Goods Sold

Cost of goods sold is determined by the invoice price of the merchandise sold plus transportation plus alteration or assembly costs. Note that those costs involved in preparing merchandise to be sold must be added to the invoice price. Alterations, such

Gross Sales	$911,880,000	
– Returns, Allowances & Discounts	17,880,000	
NET SALES	**$894,000,000**	**100%**
Cost of Goods Sold		
Opening Inventory	291,700,000	
Purchases	444,140,000	
+ Inward Freight	70,000,000	
Total Goods Handled	805,840,000	
– Closing Inventory	260,500,000	
NET COST OF GOODS SOLD	**$545,340,000**	**61%**
GROSS MARGIN	**$348,660,000**	**39%**
OPERATING EXPENSES	**$312,900,000**	**35%**
Direct	$175,000,000	
Indirect	$137,900,000	
NET PROFIT BEFORE TAXES	**$35,760,000**	**4%**

FIGURE 8.1 Perry's income statement for last year

as hemming of men's trousers, or assembly of a microwave cart would be considered a cost of merchandise or goods sold.

Invoice amount of merchandise sold	$3,000
+ Alterations	$250
+ Freight	$50
– 8% cash discount	$240
= Cost of goods sold	$3,060

Gross Margin

The difference between the net sales and the cost of goods sold is gross margin. This is often the bottom line for departmental buyers who have little or no control over store operating expenses. Buyers are given a gross margin percentage and dollars to achieve and are evaluated by comparing the actual versus planned gross margin percentage and dollars.

Net sales	$50,000	100%
– Cost of goods sold	$25,000	50%
= Gross margin	$25,000	50%

Operating Expenses

Operating expenses are the costs attributed to the operations of the organization. Salary, rent, and utilities are operating expenses. There are two types of operating expenses: indirect (or fixed) and direct (or variable). Your perspective is that of a retail buyer who operates the department as an individual profit center.

Fixed expenses are those that do not vary from month to month. For the departmental buyer, these include upper-management salaries, insurance, utilities, and so on. *Variable expenses* are expenses the buyer can manipulate, such as departmental salaries, advertising, and rent per square foot of allotted floor space.

Net sales	$50,000	100%
– Cost of goods sold	$25,000	50%
= Gross margin	$25,000	50%
– Operating expenses	$20,000	
Direct	$12,000	
Indirect	$8,000	
= Operating profit	$5,000	

Net Other Income

Net other income is earnings generated from sources other than the sale of merchandise. Examples might be interest charges from a store's credit card operations, interest earned on investments, or stock dividends. These components combine to create an operating or income statement as shown here:

Gross sales	$105,000	
− Customer returns & allowances	$5,000	
= Net sales	$100,000	100%
− Cost of goods sold	$50,000	50%
= Gross margin	$50,000	50%
− Operating expenses	$45,000	45%
= Operating profit	$5,000	5%
+ Other income	$1,000	1%
= Net profit	$6,000	6%

Note that both dollars and percentages are used to express the components. Percentages provide a better point of comparison than do dollars.

For example, Company A generates $10,000 in profit, whereas Company B generates $8,000 in profit. Which one is operating more efficiently? We must look beyond dollars (see the following example) to understand the complete profit picture.

Company B earned 8 percent profit, while Company A earned 5 percent; therefore, we could surmise that Company B operates more efficiently, or at least effectively.

	COMPANY A		COMPANY B	
Net sales	$200,000	100%	$100,000	100%
− Cost of goods sold	$100,000	50%	$50,000	50%
= Gross margin	$100,000	50%	$50,000	50%
− Expenses	$90,000	45%	$42,000	42%
= Profit	$10,000	5%	$8,000	8%

The goal of the buyer is to increase earnings. Three ways to improve profit are:

* Increase sales

* Decrease cost of goods

* Decrease expenses

Retailers often speak of sales as the top line and the net income/profit as the bottom line. It seems as if the best plan would be to balance the top line and bottom line, but a company may also decide on a strategy to aggressively maximize sales at the expense of a lower profit, or focus on increasing profit without growing sales. A buyer may have an aggressive plan to increase sales, but in the process, take too many markdowns or too low of a markup, resulting in a lower percentage of profit. It is also possible for a buyer to be so conservative in maintaining a healthy markup on merchandise that sales do not increase significantly. By increasing the markup on merchandise, a buyer can achieve higher profit margins on merchandise sold. To improve profit, buyers may look beyond merchandise and focus on cutting departmental expenses.

One example of cutting expenses is to take fewer trips domestically and overseas. However, in planning sales and profit, it is important to also remember that dollars are taken to the bank, not percentages. For example, a buyer may have a best-selling item that is performing well at a margin of 54 percent. That same item, offered at a lower key price point, could significantly increase sales, providing more profit dollars even though it may be at a lower markup.

600 units × $60 retail = $36,000 sales at regular price
600 units × $27.50 cost = $16,500 cost of goods
= $19,500, 54% gross margin

2,400 units × $49.99 retail = $119,976 sales at key price point
2,400 units × $27.50 cost = $66,000 cost of goods
= $53,976, 45% gross margin

In this example, the item made more profit dollars by selling more units at a lower price point, even though the percentage of margin is lower. This assumes the buyer pays the same price as the regular buy. When a buyer recognizes that an item is a good seller and has the potential to achieve higher sales if offered at a lower key price point, the buyer often goes back to the vendor to negotiate a lower price for buying a larger volume of merchandise, hence lowering the cost of goods.

For more detailed examples of income statements, search the Internet to find the most recent income statements for department stores and compare them.

## CHAPTER 9

The Buyer's Role in Product Development

IN THIS CHAPTER, YOU WILL LEARN:

* The changes in the buyer's responsibilities with regard to product development
* The steps of the product development process as they impact the buyer
* How private label merchandise improves gross margin
* The skills and knowledge a buyer must have or develop to meet the demands of the product development process

As the gross margin and the bottom line have become the driving force of businesses, buyers must look for new ways of creating a competitive edge in the marketplace. Developing merchandise specifically for their ***target customer*** under a ***private label (store brand)*** or with exclusive distribution rights has become the buyers' way of increasing their profit margins while giving their customers exactly what they want.

BACKGROUND

With the vertical integration and horizontal growth of retailers, globalization, economies of scale in both retailing and apparel manufacturing, and market specialization, the role of the retail buyer has changed dramatically in the last 25 years. These market changes have precipitated major changes in the responsibilities of today's buyer.

Today, buyers must have comprehensive knowledge of their target customer, including demographics, psychographics, style, color, and fabric preferences, as well as price points that the market will bear. Buyers must stay current with trends in styling, fabric, and fiber development, quality control and production issues, market information, domestic and international current events, and socioeconomic trends that may affect the purchase of their merchandise or the development of a new category. Armed with extensive market research and knowledge of both consumer preferences and the market, the buyer is ready to take part in the many interrelated steps of the product development process.

BRANDING

New product lines must be developed with a position or competitive edge in mind from the very beginning of the process. A private label line must fill a niche with respect to the current branded merchandise assortment, and it must have special appeal to that same consumer, offering similar personality, quality, and style while being more competitively priced than the branded merchandise. Branding is a multifaceted process that goes beyond the development of a distinctive product and extends to creating an identity or image for the entity of the brand. Branding is a promise to deliver the consistent quality and innovation expected by the store's target customer. Luxury brands are expected to deliver exceptional quality and ultra-contemporary styles, whereas a mainstream brand delivers less cutting-edge fashion at a much lower price.

Branding is the creation of an identity through the use of logos (CC for Chanel), identifiable colors (Tiffany blue), or iconic styles (Burberry trench coat or plaid), and the creation of a lifestyle that consumers attempt to emulate through the purchase of the brand. Today's buyers are a major part of the development of these private label brands, because they understand the consumer and are able to spot an opportunity to create a brand that their consumers will find appealing. Working with executives and creative personnel, buyers work to develop a new brand's position or competitive edge, its promise or values, and its identity through the creation of distinctive images and a brand name. For example, Saks Fifth Avenue developed a menswear private label brand called the *Men's Collection*, and according to *Off the Cuff*, Saks' reasoning was based on the following statement: "Luxury labels are pushing retailers for higher profit margins. Private labels are a balancing factor that brings up-market shoppers a more affordable alternative but only when (1) actual quality, in both manufacturing and design, and (2) perceived value are accepted."

PRODUCT PLANNING

Product planning is the next step in the product development process. Simply stated, buyers must determine the right merchandise for their consumer. Based on research, market knowledge, instinct, and experience, the buyer and the design team (depending on the size of the organization) brainstorm the attributes and styling of the upcoming product line. This meeting might include the discussion of aspects such as style and color trends, silhouettes, fabrication, customer preferences, competing brands, pricing, projected unit sales volume, and innovative ideas to obtain a competitive advantage over branded merchandise. Using the information from this meeting, design and concept boards are developed and presented for several product lines or collections for an upcoming season. Depending on the classification of merchandise and the type and size of the organization, as few as two product lines could be developed or as many as twelve might be created to ensure a constant flow of new merchandise on a monthly basis. However, most organizations develop four to five seasonal product lines in a given year for specific departments or classifications.

Salability

At the presentation of the design or concept boards, buyers are primarily concerned with the salability of the merchandise with regard to the brand. Their focus is on getting the right merchandise to the customer at the right price and at the right time. The previous year's best-selling items from both the private label brand and its competitors are reviewed, and lost sales from underplanning are discussed. The team of designers and merchandisers edit the proposed collections and designs, and they discuss the fabrication of each of the merchandise groups. They determine the number of collections needed and which collection will be delivered to the sales floor first.

Fabric

Fabric selection is based on characteristics that the consumer desires, as well as the cost and availability of the fabric or an alternative selection. This is where a buyer's knowledge of textiles becomes critical. Buyers must understand performance characteristics such as wearability, care requirements, construction constraints, drape, colorfastness, and dye issues. They must also be aware of sourcing issues such as country quotas, if the fabric is to be imported, and time constraints related to the shipping costs to the factory for production. Price and terms and the availability of fabric are key to meeting production deadlines and profit goals.

Specification and Costing Sheets

From this point, samples or prototypes are made before a final review of that season's product assortment. *Specification (spec) sheets* or technical drawings are developed to outline fabrication, costing, *sourcing*, and specific production notes or instructions.

The spec sheets are a critical part of the buyer's job, because they ensure that the merchandise is made correctly. They are the blueprints for the factory to build the merchandise to the buyer's exact specifications. These sheets include the exact measurements for each size and how those measurements are made (e.g., ½ inch from the neckline), the number of sizes to be made (e.g., sizes 3–13), the assigned style number, the tolerance of deviation from the specifications (e.g., no more than ¼ inch), the cutting instructions, the detail instructions for topstitching or pocket placement, the labeling, and the detailed sketch of the item (see Figure 9.1). Details are the key to production success, and the buyer is the detail person in the product development process.

The specification sheets are also the key to quality control and assurance. The buyer is focused on many quality issues, including pattern and fit of the garment, construction, finishing, and, of course, fabrication. A first sample is tried on a fitting model to check for fit and to make any necessary adjustments to the pattern before it goes into production. A buyer must also check the finishing of seams, the type and number of stitches per inch, as well as the lining, buttonholes, zippers, and the like. Placement of pockets and/or trim and repeat patterns within the fabric all must be checked for accuracy. This sample must be reproducible in a factory with minimal room for error. The sample garment and production garment should be identical. Sometimes buyers travel to factories to check production and ensure quality of the finished goods.

Costing sheets are also developed, often by the buyer, detailing all expenses involved in the manufacture of the goods. These worksheets are also used to determine the price at which the goods will retail. Information on the cost sheets includes the type of fabric, the manufacturer of that fabric, the amount of fabric, and the cost per yard of fabric per unit. Trim and ***findings***—notions such as zippers, labels, buttons, and/or belts—are specified and priced. Labor costs are calculated, including marking, grading, cutting, finishing, and construction costs. If the merchandise is imported, then import duties and additional shipping costs must be calculated.

From this final figure, a retail price can be calculated based on a targeted gross margin percentage or markup. If the proposed retail price of the merchandise is too high for the target customer, then the buyer or merchandiser must make adjustments to make the item more salable. The buyer may suggest different buttons or a less expensive fabric, even a different factory or country of origin, while still maintaining the integrity of the original design concept. See Figure 9.2 for a domestic costing sheet and Figure 9.3 for an import product sheet.

PERRY'S

MEN'S WEAR							
SIZE	34	36	38	40	42	44	46
CHEST	36	38	40	42	44	46	48
BUST							
BUST FRONT ARC							
WAIST	30	32	34	36	38	40	42
HIPS @ 4"	35	37	39	41	43	45	47
HIPS @ 8"	37	39	41	43	45	47	49
LENGTH WAIST BACK	16 ¾	17	17 ¼	17 ½	17 ¾	18	18 ¼
LENGTH WAIST FRONT	14 ¼	14 ½	14 3/4	15	15 ¼	15 1/2	15 ¾
ACROSS SHOULDER	16 ½	17	17 ½	18	18 ½	19	19 ½
ACROSS BACK @ 4"	15 ½	16	16 ½	17	17 ½	18	18 ½
ACROSS CHEST @ 1 1/2"	15	15 ½	16	16 ½	17	17 ½	18
DIAPHRAGM UNDER BUST							
DIAPHRAGM MIDWAY							
SHOULDER							
BUST AROUND NECK							
NECK	14 ¾	15 1/4	15 ¾	16 1/4	16 ¾	17 ¼	17 ¾
CROTCH W.W.	27	28	29	30	31	32	33
MAX THIGH	22	23	24	25	26	27	28
MIDDLE THIGH							
KNEE	15	15 ½	16	16 ½	17	17 ½	18
CALF	14	14 ½	15	15 ½	16	16 ½	17
ANKLE							
ANKLE LENGTH							
WAIST TO KNEE							
WAIST TO FLOOR							
CROTCH HEIGHT—ANKLE	29 ⅝	29 ¾	29 ⅞	30	30 ⅛	30 ¼	30 ⅜
KNEE HEIGHT							
ACROSS BUST							
B.M.S.							

FIGURE 9.1 Perry's specification sheet for menswear

PERRY'S

COSTING SHEET

Piece Goods Cost/Yard		$ 9.00		
Freight to Sponger & Contractor	+	$ 0.50		
Sponging Cost/Yard	+	$ 0.35		
Cost per Yard	=	$ 9.85		
Yield	×	3.5		
TOTAL PIECE GOODS COST			$ 34.48	
CMT	+	$ 45.00		
Upcharges	+	$ 2.00		
(DB, plaids, elbow patches, etc.)				
TOTAL Production COSTs			$ 47.00	
Hanger	+	$ 0.60		
Labels	+	$ 0		
Poly Bag	+	$ 0		
Hanger Box	+	$ 0		
Freight	+	$ 0.50		
Trademark Charge	+	$ 1.00		
Additional Financing	+	$ 1.00		
TOTAL Other COSTS			$ 3.10	
TOTAL COST DELIVERED			$ 84.58	
UNIT RETAIL			$ 219.95	$ 199.95
INITIAL MARK-ON			61.50%	57.70%

FIGURE 9.2 Perry's costing sheet

PERRY'S

Date:	1/15/09
Dept:	Gifts
Buyer:	K. Smith
Phone:	703-555-1212
E-mail:	ksmith@perrys.com

Season: Fall 2009

Manufacturer Name & Address:

Domore

Contact: Christina

Phone:

Fax:

E-mail:

Agent Name:		**Commission:**	
Item #:	43278	**Description:** Decorative black metal plate rack with 4 nautical asst. 8" plates, vertical, 39.75" L × 11.5" W	
Port:	Shenzhen		
Lead Time:	90 days		
Minimum:	1,200 units	**Materials/Fiber Content % Weight:** Metal plate rack, powder coated; ceramic plates	
Cube:	3.0		
Inner:	1		
Master:	4	**Tariff Number:** 7326.2000.70	
40' Container Qty:	2,664	**Carton Meas. L: W: H:**	
20' Container Qty:		**UPC#:** 055176432780	
Unit of Measure:	each		
FOB U.S. $ Cost:	$6.75		
Freight:	1.50	$2.00 per cu.ft.	
Duty:	26.0%	3.90%	
Misc.:	0.34	5% of F.O.B. cost	
Landed Cost:	8.85		
Retail:	$24.99	**64.6% margin**	color photo here
Units Ordering:	2,664		

FIGURE 9.3 Perry's import product sheet

Another critical element of the buyer's job in some companies is the sourcing of all the elements that make up a finished product. The buyer may be responsible for procuring all of the fabric, trims, and buttons and must coordinate the delivery of these items to the factory where the garment or item is to be produced. Considering the global nature of the apparel and accessory business and the gift industry, these different components probably come from all over the world, and the coordination of their timely arrival is critical to production deadlines. Because of the competitive nature of the fashion industry and its labor-intensive product, sourcing has become a global endeavor. Labor costs are significantly lower in certain parts of the world, and government initiatives encourage the use of foreign factories, fabrics, and findings.

Buyers must be knowledgeable of *quotas* such as the ***General Agreement on Tariffs and Trade (GATT)*** and now the ***World Trade Organization (WTO)*** guidelines. They must also understand how and what duties are charged on imported products and the numerous agreements impacting trade, such as the ***North American Free Trade Agreement (NAFTA)*** and the ***Dominion Republic–Central America Free Trade Agreement (CFTA-DR)***.

Buyers also must stay abreast of political and economic issues that might affect production at a factory in another part of the world, and they must be sensitive to human rights issues related to work, such as child labor and health, and safety issues. Many retailers, such as Kmart and Wal-Mart, have received negative publicity because the factories used to produce their merchandise violated the human rights of local workers in developing nations. This is another reason why buyers often visit factories in other parts of the world.

Testing

Another issue of concern for the buyer is the testing of fabrication and construction of the merchandise to be manufactured. The buyer must have the fabric tested to make sure it meets the specifications detailed on the spec sheets. Numerous test services or facilities will test fabric flammability, fabric performance, and actual performance of the garment. These critical issues ensure the salability of the merchandise and its entry into the United States.

Labeling

Labeling requirements are also of concern to buyers. U.S. law requires that all apparel merchandise sold in the United States be labeled with fabric content, country of origin, and care instructions. The placement of this label is also critical to the wearability of the garment. For an example of private label guidelines for label placement, go to https://www.saksincorporated.com/vendorrelations/documents /saksfifthavenueoff5th-labelplacementguide11-81.pdf to see Saks Fifth Avenue's label placement guide for vendors.

SHIPPING

The product mix requires that the buyer get the merchandise to the consumer at the right time. Shipping arrangements are important, especially for goods made outside of the United States. The buyer must determine whether the goods should be shipped by air or boat, and the cost will impact the profitability of the goods. The documentation that must accompany imported goods is significant and includes such items as quota visa, commercial invoice, bill of lading, packing slip, and surety bond.

If any of the documentation is incorrect or missing, the shipment could be held up for weeks, which could negatively affect the salability of the goods because of the seasonal nature of fashion. Import agents often manage much of this process, because they are closer to the merchandise or are in frequent contact with the factory. These agents are usually fluent in the native language of the region where the factory is located, and they are also specialists in exporting goods from the country of origin to the United States.

Technology

As product development buyers' responsibilities continue to evolve, so does the technology that assists them in managing the process. ***Computer-aided design (CAD) systems*** allow merchandise to be created on a two- and three-dimensional basis, and to create patterns that will account for fabric properties and anomalies. Textile prints can be created and placed on specific garments to maximize fabric use and efficiency. A factory in Japan can show a prototype garment with a choice of fabric, findings, and style variations via a networked system, live telecast, or downloadable images from the Internet. Changes can be made immediately, and communication difficulties (e.g., language differences) can be clarified.

Product management systems help the buyer create product development calendars, style descriptions, cost sheets, specification sheets, quality control data, vendor quote analyses, and standard measurement tables, as well as manage sourcing and transportation information. The buyer must master new technologies to remain competitive in an industry that is demanding shorter and shorter ***lead times*** and delivery times of new merchandise.

SUMMARY

Product development has added an exciting but demanding dimension to the buyer's job. Not only does it allow the buyer to be more creative, but it also requires in-depth knowledge of branding principles, production cycles, product construction, and fabrication. Buyers must recognize great design, but they also understand the limitations placed by financial constraints, gross margin projections, international quotas, global economic conditions, and current events. A buyer must be sensitive to cross-cultural nuances that can make or break a deal while negotiating a smart bargain that creates a win-win situation for both organizations. Today's buyer must be detail oriented, technologically savvy, culturally sensitive, and creatively inclined.

## CHAPTER 10

Career Opportunities in Retail Buying

IN THIS CHAPTER, YOU WILL LEARN:

* The different types of buying careers and career paths
* The entry-, mid-, and upper-level buying positions
* The roles, skills, and responsibilities of buying positions

This chapter details many job titles and corresponding job requirements available in retail buying. Beginning with entry-level, trainee positions and concluding at the level of general merchandise manager, it is a helpful section for the student. Other aspects are touched upon as well—the broadening areas of buying, the availability of trainee programs, and the opportunities in buying groups.

OVERVIEW

Although the role of the retail buyer generally remains consistent from small to large stores, the number of positions that assist buying activities varies. The larger the store operation, the more levels of opportunity are available. In larger corporations, buyers may be accountable for as much as $50 million or more in sales volume. Retail buying jobs have broadened to include more positions in merchandise analysis and planning to assist the buyer in controlling high volume. In many stores, the career path to the level of buyer and above weaves back and forth between the store operation and the buying division. Focusing on the buying division, many operations further divide responsibility between buying and merchandising/planning.

Numerous department and chain stores recruit college graduates to join their executive training programs. College graduates are hired on an executive level and receive on-the-job training for entry-level executive positions. At Neiman Marcus, the Executive Development Program is a 12-week training program of classroom instruction and buying office rotations, leading to a full-time position as an assistant buyer upon completion.

Internships are another way to join a company and receive on-the-job training while the student is in college, before graduating. Internships often lead to full-time employment. Internships can be in management, merchandise and planning, product development, marketing, or other related divisions of a retail store. Nordstrom is just one of the department stores that offers opportunities for internships in various divisions within the company for college juniors and seniors. The program is nine to ten weeks from June through August.

Merchandise assistant, *merchandise coordinator*, *analyst*, and *allocator* are some of the typical entry-level jobs for college graduates in the buying division.

Merchandise Assistant, Merchandise Coordinator

All buyers require administrative support. Clerical duties characteristic of this job include distributing store orders, tracking orders to be sure they are delivered on time, instituting markdowns on seasonal and slow-moving items, obtaining samples for advertising, and handling return-to-vendor merchandise. At HSN, the television shopping network, a merchandise assistant is also responsible for transporting samples to the Quality Assurance department for quality assurance testing and managing the sample room with product for upcoming shows.

Qualifications required for the position are strong organizational and communication skills, high motivation, and the ability to handle multiple tasks. Computer experience in Excel and Word is essential. At Target Corporation, new merchandise coordinators enroll in a six-week training course for their positions. Courses are available to strengthen computer skills and to learn management techniques.

Business Analyst, Merchandise Analyst, or Merchandise Allocator

The analyst or allocator is responsible for managing inventory and allocating merchandise to the stores. An important duty is to review and reorder basic stock. Another task is to detect bestsellers and identify slow-moving items. Sales and stock are analyzed to forecast sales projections and plan assortments. The analyst or allocator communicates with vendors, checks on orders, and exchanges information on stock and sales. At Target Corporation, a business analyst advances to senior business analyst on the career path.

The entry-level position of business analyst, merchandise analyst, or merchandise allocator requires a college degree or previous retail or business experience. Qualifications of the job include strong analytical, decision-making, planning, and problem-solving skills. The candidate should possess good communication and organizational skills and exhibit strong initiative. The next step for a merchandise analyst at Lord & Taylor is assistant buyer.

Planner

Within the merchandising/planning track, the role of the planner is to plan and regulate inventory. By analyzing past sales and inventory history, the planner forecasts trends to maximize sales and profit.

In Federated Department Stores, such as Macy's and Bloomingdale's, the planner works with the buying team and individual store locations to develop assortment plans for a core vendor, specific area, or department. The planner identifies key items, plans purchases, allocates merchandise to appropriate locations, and monitors stock levels for replenishment. Reorders for stock replenishment are presented to the buyer. A planner at Saks makes sure the right merchandise is at the right store at the right time. The planner collaborates with the buyer to manage the inventory, increase sales, and improve margins.

A planner at HSN plans the strategy and forecasts inventory for shows. Together with the buying and programming team, the planner helps identify new business and key items. Following the show, a recap is presented to the buyer. The planner handles reorders and disposition of remaining goods after the show.

Qualifications for this position include excellent written and oral communication skills, detail orientation, strong analytical abilities, and computer competency in Word and Excel. Both Macy's and Bloomingdale's offer planning executive trainee programs. A trainee can advance from assistant planner to associate planner to planner.

Manager of Planning and Distribution

A *manager of planning and distribution (MPD)* works with the divisional merchandise manager (DMM) and buying team and oversees a team of planners. The manager provides guidance for the merchandise division to effectively plan, distribute, and monitor inventory levels by store location. The goal is to maximize sales, maintain proper turnover, and increase profit. The manager works with the team to formulate strategies to accomplish set objectives. Depending on the store, the title for this position may vary.

Qualifications for this position are four to seven years' experience as a planner or buyer and several years' experience as a supervisor. The manager must have excellent analytical and communication skills.

Director of Distribution and Planning

The *director of distribution and planning (DDP)* supervises the MPD and planning team. This position is accountable for achieving sales and profit goals for a specific business. The director assists in developing strategies and seeking opportunities to meet financial objectives and location plans. The director works closely with the buying team to direct assortment planning.

The requirements for a DDP are four to seven years of retail planning or buying and several years of supervising a team. As in other planning jobs, a director must have strong analytical skills, good written and oral communication skills, and an ability to form partnerships and communicate with all levels of the organization.

Assistant Buyer

The *assistant buyer* manages the buying office and supports the buyer in all aspects of business. Depending on the buyer's volume and breadth of responsibility, the assistant may undertake buying for a classification. Assistants are accountable for monitoring delivery of purchase orders and communicating with both the distribution center and the vendors. The buyer relies on the assistant to analyze the business and prepare recaps and reports. Stock levels are examined for appropriate distribution. The assistant advises the buyer and stores of bestsellers and key items. Other tasks are to identify slow sellers and seasonal merchandise and plan markdowns within the budget. Assistants take part in advertising preparation by completing ad requests, obtaining samples from vendors, submitting items for ads at advertising meetings, proofing ads, and recapping results. Depending on the proximity of the market, the buyer may ask the assistant buyer to attend markets.

An assistant buyer must be able to work in a fast-paced environment, be detail oriented and organized, possess superb analytical skills, and have strong oral and written communication skills. Computer experience is required, with proficiency in Word and Excel.

Associate Buyer, Senior Assistant Buyer

The next step toward buyer is the position of *associate buyer* or *senior assistant buyer*, depending on what title the store may use. The associate or senior assistant is accountable for managing and buying for an assigned area. This includes developing pricing and promotional strategy for the area, formulating the dollar merchandise plan, shopping the market to identify trends and merchandise opportunities, and negotiating with vendors. The associate or senior assistant buyer works with planners on assortments and distribution. Recommendations for merchandise presentation are presented to the visual merchandising team.

For this position, the candidate should be detail-oriented, have strong analytical skills, be effective in oral and written communication skills, have knowledge of basic retail math and computer skills, and be able to work well with others. At least 18 months or more of experience as an assistant buyer are required.

Buyer, Senior Buyer

The buyer is responsible for planning, managing, and achieving financial objectives for one or more departments of the store. The company holds the buyer accountable for meeting sales, markdowns, gross margin, and turnover goals. The buyer develops the merchandising and marketing strategy for the area of business, supervises the procurement of merchandise, builds relationships with vendors, monitors performance of merchandise and vendors, and provides direction for visual presentation. Buyers work closely with the planning team to create proper assortment plans and to advise on distribution. Training of assistant and associate buyers is also a task for the buyer.

To become a buyer, two or more years of experience is required, depending on the size of the business area and the store organization. Qualifications include abilities in strategic planning and forecasting, strong analytical skills, good written and oral communication skills, and the ability to effectively communicate with all levels of management. Buyers need to be detail-oriented, have a sense of urgency, and be adept in handling multiple tasks.

Divisional Merchandise Manager

Buyers report to a divisional merchandise manager (DMM). The DMM oversees the implementation of the merchandise strategy and financial goals for specific merchandise divisions, such as menswear or home furnishings. The DMM directs the buyers in merchandise selection and purchasing for all areas within the division. The DMM provides the vision and ensures that the strategy and goals meet company plans. The planning team looks to the DMM for direction in assortment planning and location distribution. The DMM works with buyers to build their relationships with vendors and provides support and promotes the growth of the buyer. The person in this position must also be aware of competitors and their strengths and weaknesses.

Experience of four or more years in buying or merchandising and several years of supervising a team are required for the position of DMM. The DMM must exhibit strong leadership and negotiation skills. The person should be organized, able to compete in a fast-paced environment, demonstrate strong analytical skills and excellent oral and written communication skills, and have the ability to build teams and develop partnerships.

General Merchandise Manager

The general merchandise managers (GMMs) oversee more than one division, with the DMM reporting to them. Typically, a store has a GMM for soft goods, such as clothing and bedding, and a GMM for durable goods, such as household appliances. Duties and qualifications are the same as those of the DMM.

Buying Groups and Services

Some larger department stores and chains operate their own buying and sourcing organizations. Macy's Merchandising Group employs a design and production team to design and source private label brands for the Macy's, Inc., stores. The group also works together with buyers to source product from national brands. Target Sourcing Services/AMC sources product from overseas for Target buyers. Design and merchandising services include product development to production of merchandise.

Many stores rely on the expertise of external buying groups and services to provide guidance in retail buying and merchandising. The Doneger Group and Kurt Salmon Associates are two well-known consulting companies that provide trend information and merchandising planning for their customers. Li and Fung Limited is a sourcing operation based in Hong Kong that sources apparel and home furnishings product from overseas for customers. For additional information on buying groups and services, go to www.apparelsearch.com/buying_groups.htm.

THE INTERNET

To research job opportunities through the Internet, use a search engine such as Google. Type the name of the store or buying organization of interest into the search box. Most websites have a tab for careers within that company and an online application. You will find additional job opportunities other than those listed in the text. For example, there may be opportunities in visual merchandising, marketing, operations, catalog, and online divisions. Specific jobs are too numerous to list all of them. Another good source for job opportunities is the classified section of trade magazines. For a general search of career openings, you may find the following websites helpful:

About.com
www.careerbuilder.com
www.indeed.com
LinkedIn.com
www.monster.com
www.simplyhired.com
www.stylecareers.com
us.fashionjobs.com
www.24seventalent.com

Website Resources

Following is a selection of organizations and their corresponding Internet addresses relating to retail buying. Readers may wish to use a search engine such as Google or a directory such as Yahoo! to find additional relevant websites. Be aware that new sites are launched constantly, while others disappear just as quickly.

Buying Groups and Major Department and Luxury Retail Stores

Barney's: www.barneys.com

Belk Stores: www.belk.com

Bergdorf Goodman: www.bergdorfgoodman.com

Bloomingdale's: www.bloomingdales.com

Bon-Ton: www.bonton.com

Boscov's: www.boscovs.com

Burberry: www.burberry.com

Cartier: www.cartier.com

Chanel: www.chanel.com

Coach: www.coach.com

Dillard's: www.dillards.com

The Doneger Group: www.doneger.com

Elder-Beerman: www.elder-beerman.com

Fendi: www.fendi.com

FredMeyer: www.fredmeyer.com

Gucci: www.gucci.com

Hermes: www.hermes.com

Henri Bendel: www.henribendel.com

HSN: www.hsn.com

Lord and Taylor: www.lordandtaylor.com

Louis Vuitton: www.louisvuitton.com

Macy's: www.macysinc.com

Neiman Marcus: www.neimanmarcus.com

Nordstrom: www.nordstrom.com

Prada: www.prada.com

QVC: www.iqvc.com

Saks: www.saksfifthavenue.com

Stage Stores: www.stagestores.com

Industry Resources

American Wool Council: www.americanwool.org

American Apparel and Footwear Association:
www.apparelandfootwear.org

Apparel Search: www.apparelsearch.com

Cotton Incorporated: www.cottoninc.com

National Retail Federation: www.nrf.com

Pantone: www.pantone.com

Market Centers and Trade Show Information

AmericasMart: www.americasmart.com

Buylink: www.buylink.com

CaliforniaMart: www.californiamart.com

Capsule: www.capsuleshow.com

Children's Club:
www.enkshows.com/childrensclub

Coeur: www.coeurshow.com

Dallas Market Center:
www.dallasmarketcenter.com

The Fashion Center: www.fashioncenter.com

Fashion Coterie: www.enkshows.com

Fashion Week Las Vegas:
www.fashionweek-lasvegas.com

George Little Management: www.glmshows.com

MAGIC (Men's Apparel Guild in California): www.magiconline.com

Merchandise Mart Properties: www.mmart.com

Moda: www.modashows.com

MRket: www.mrketshow.com

NYC Fashion: nycfashioninfo.com

PoolTrade Show: www.magiconline.com

Project: www.projectshow.com

WeConnectFashion.: www.weconnectfashion.com

World Market Center, Las Vegas: www.lasvegasmarket.com

Trade Publications, Websites, and Trend Information

Accessories: www.accessoriesmagazine.com

Accessory Merchandising: www.accessorymerchandising.com

Apparel News: www.apparelnews.net

Bloomsbury: www.bloomsbury.com

Business of Fashion: www.businessoffashion.com/

DNR: www.dnrnews.com

The Doneger Group: www.doneger.com

Earnshaw's: www.earnshaws.com

Fairchild Publications: www.fairchildpub.com

Fashion Snoops: www.fashionsnoops.com

FN Platform: www.magiconline.com/fn-platform

Furniture Style: www.furniturestyle.com

Giftbeat: www.giftbeat.com

Gifts & Decorative Accessories: www.giftsanddec.com

Giftware News: www.giftwarenews.com

Home Accents Today (HAT): www.homeaccentstoday.com

Home Furnishings News (hfn): www.hfnmag.com

Home Textiles Today (HTT): www.homeandtextilestoday.com

Infomat Fashion: www.fashion.infomat.com

Just Style: www.just-style.com

Kids Today: www.kidstodayonline.com

Label Networks: www.labelnetworks.com

Modem Online: www.modemonline.com

National Retail Federation: www.nrf.com

Stores: www.stores.org

Stylesight: www.stylesight.com

The Trend Curve: www.trendcurve.com

Trend Stop: www.trendstop.com?

Trend Zine: www.fashioninformation.com

WeAr Global Magazine: www.wear-magazine.com

Worth Global Source Network: www.wgsn.com

Women's Wear Daily (WWD): www.wwd.com

WWDMen's: www.wwd.com/menswear-news

Consumer Demographics, Psychographics, Marketing

Advertising Age: www.adage.com

American Fact Finder: www.factfinder2.census.gov

About.Com: Retail Industry: www.retailindustry.about.com

Bureau of Economic Analysis GDP: www.bea.gov

Bureau of Labor Statistics Consumer Price Index: www.bls.gov/cpi/home.htm

Bureau of Labor Statistics Producer Price Index: www.bls.gov/ppi/home.htm

KnowThis.com, Marketing Virtual Library: www.knowthis.com

Nielson: www.nielson.com

SRI Consulting Business Intelligence: www.sric-bi.com/VALS/

Unity Marketing: www.unitymarketing.com

US Census Bureau: www.census.gov/

Retailing Formulas

Planned Sales Increase/Decrease

Dollar increase = LY sales × Planned % increase

Dollar increase	TY planned sales
+ LY sales	− LY actual sales
= Planned sales	= Sales increase

Planned Sales Increase Percentage

$$\text{Percentage increase} = \frac{\text{Dollar increase}}{\text{LY actual sales}}$$

Stock-to-Sales Ratio

$$\text{Stock-to-sales ratio} = \frac{\text{Retail stock at a given time}}{\text{Sales for the period}}$$

BOM Stock

BOM stock = Planned sales × Stock-to-sales ratio

Turnover

$$\text{Turnover} = \frac{\text{Net sales for period}}{\text{Average inventory or stock for same period}}$$

Average Stock

$$\text{Average stock} = \frac{\text{BOM stock for the given period}}{\text{\# of inventories (BOM stock)}}$$

Average Stock for 6 Months

$$\text{Average stock} = \frac{\text{Sum of 6 BOM stocks + Ending stock}}{7 \text{ (6 BOM stocks + Ending stock (EOM))}}$$

Average Stock for 12 months

$$\text{Average stock} = \frac{\text{Sum of 12 BOM stocks} + \text{Ending stock (EOM)}}{13 \,(12 \text{ BOM stocks} + \text{Ending stock (EOM)})}$$

Markup

Retail price − Cost = Markup

Markup %

$$\text{Markup \%} = \frac{(\text{Retail price} - \text{cost})}{\text{Retail price}}$$

Planned Purchases

Planned sales
+ Planned EOM stock
+ Planned markdowns
− Planned BOM stock
─────────────────
= Planned purchases at retail

Planned Purchases at Cost

Planned purchases at cost = Planned purchases at retail × (1 − Markup%)

Retail

Retail = Cost × (1 − Markup %)

Open-to-buy

Planned purchases
− Outstanding purchase orders not yet delivered
─────────────────
= Open-to-buy

Open-to-buy at Cost

Open-to-buy at cost = Open-to-buy at retail × (1 − Markup %)

Sales Volume

Sales volume = Unit retail price × Number of units sold

Net Sales

Gross sales
− Customer returns, allowances, and discounts
= Net sales

Cost of Goods Sold

Invoice amount of merchandise sold
+ Alterations
+ Freight
− Cash Discount
= Cost of Goods Sold

Gross Margin

Net sales
− Cost of goods sold
= Gross margin

Total Operating Expenses

Direct expenses
+ Indirect expenses
= Total operating expenses

Sales Recap

Pre = ad on = hand units/dollars
− Post = ad on = hand units/dollars
= Total units/dollars sold

$$\frac{\text{Total units/dollars sold}}{\text{Pre = ad on = hand units/dollars}} = \text{Percentage of sell-through}$$

Glossary

assistant buyer The assistant buyer manages the buying office and supports the buyer in all aspects of business. Depending on the volume of the buyer and breadth of responsibility, the assistant may undertake buying for a classification.

associate buyer The associate buyer or senior assistant is accountable for managing and buying for an assigned area in the buying office.

assortment plan The breakdown of merchandise by classification.

average stock (average inventory) The sum of the retail inventories divided by the number of inventories in the period examined (month, season, or year).

balanced stock Stock sufficient to meet planned sales without overstocking the department.

bulk estimate An estimate of total units per style that a store buyer might purchase. The estimate of the style may not be detailed by color, size, or individual branch store for shipping.

business analyst The analyst or allocator is a position in the buying office that is responsible for managing inventory and allocating merchandise to the stores.

buyer The buyer is responsible for planning, managing, and achieving financial objectives for one or more departments of the retail store.

CAFTA-DR (Caribbean Free Trade Act-Dominican Republic) Signed on August 5, 2004, the United States signed the Domincan Republic-Central America-United States Free Trade Agreement with five Central American countries (Costa Rica, El Salvador, Guatemala, Honduras and Nicaragua) and the Domincan Republic creating new economic opportunities by eliminating tariffs, opening markets, reducing barriers to services and promoting transparency.

cash discount A percentage of deduction taken for paying an invoice within the specified time allowed.

classification A type of merchandise, such as dresses or skirts.

classification report A sales report provided to buyers by classification, such as sales of skirts for a specified period of time.

closeouts Merchandise that is marked down for clearance.

computer-aided design (CAD) system A computer system that allows designers to create both two- and three-dimensional designs.

cost of goods sold Determined by the invoice price of merchandise sold plus transportation plus alteration or assembly costs.

costing sheets Forms used to estimate all costs associated with the construction and production of a garment or item.

dating Amount of time allowed for payment of an invoice.

director of distribution and planning (DDP) This buying position is responsible for supervising the *MPD* and the planning team and for achieving sales and profit goals of a specific business.

divisional merchandise manager (DMM) Managerial person responsible for a group of buyers and their specific merchandise categories.

drop paper An order placed with a vendor or wholesaler, usually at a sales appointment while the buyer is in the market.

electronic data interchange (EDI) Computerized communication network used among retailer, manufacturer, and other supply chain members.

EOM dating Dating computed from the end of the month.

extra dating Allowance of a longer period to pay an invoice and still receive a discount.

findings Notions such as zippers, labels, buttons, and/or belts.

fixed expenses Costs that do not vary from month to month.

FOB Free on board.

FOB factory Delivery term whereby the store takes ownership of merchandise once the goods leave the manufacturer's factory; the store is also responsible for all freight charges and insurance.

FOB point Location where the merchandise changes ownership from manufacturer to store.

FOB store Delivery term whereby the manufacturer retains ownership of and responsibility for merchandise until it reaches the store; the manufacturer thus pays all freight charges and insurance.

General Agreement on Tariffs and Trade (GATT) An agreement (1947) among many countries to reduce trade barriers and unify trading practices. In 1995, it was replaced by the *World Trade Organization (WTO)*.

general merchandise manager (GMM) Management person responsible for specific merchandise divisions. Oversees divisional merchandise managers.

gross margin Dollar amount of profit after subtracting costs of merchandise sold from total net sales; difference between net sales and cost of goods sold.

gross sales Total sales before any adjustments for customer returns, customer allowances, and/or sales discounts.

incentive purchasing See *seasonal discount*.

landed duty paid (LDP) Total cost for imported merchandise delivered to a location that includes shipping, duty, delivery insurance and customs clearance.

lead time The period of time needed to manufacture merchandise from receipt of the order to time of delivery.

manager of planning and distribution (MPD) The MPD works with the divisional merchandise manager and buying team, and oversees a team of planners. The MPD provides guidance for the merchandise division to effectively plan, distribute, and monitor inventory levels by store location.

markdown A reduction in the retail price of an item.

market The location where vendors show and sell their merchandise to retail store buyers.

markup The dollar amount added to the cost of an item to determine the selling price to cover expenses and profit.

markup percentage In retail, the difference between the selling price and the cost expressed as a percentage of the retail.

Men's Apparel Guild in California (MAGIC) A menswear trade association that sponsors market twice a year; currently held in Las Vegas, Nevada.

merchandise allocator See *business analyst*.

merchandise analyst See *business analyst*.

merchandise assistant An assistant in the buying office who performs administrative duties. Clerical duties characteristic of this job include executing store distribution of orders, tracking orders to be sure they are delivered on time, instituting markdowns on seasonal and slow-moving items, obtaining samples for advertising, and handling *return to vendor (RTV)* merchandise.

merchandise coordinator See *merchandise assistant*.

monochronic culture People who have a preference to work on only one task at a time. Monochronic people are punctual and prefer working with a sequential plan.

negotiation Discussion between two or more people who work together to resolve a problem or come to terms on a deal, each having to give and take to reach a final agreement.

net other income Monies generated from sources other than the sale of merchandise.

North American Free Trade Agreement (NAFTA) An agreement that eliminated quotas and tariffs for goods shipped between Canada, Mexico, and the United States.

open-to-buy (OTB) The amount of money available to purchase merchandise that is not accounted for by previous purchase orders. Knowledge of OTB allows the buyer to regulate or adjust inventory levels according to actual sales.

operating expenses Costs attributed to the organization's operations.

planner Within the merchandising/planning track, the role of the planner is to plan and regulate inventory. By analyzing past sales and inventory history, the planner forecasts trends to maximize sales and profit.

polychronic culture People who have a preference to work on multiple tasks and capable of communicating with multiple persons at the same time. Polychronic people are flexible.

price line A predetermined retail price for an assortment or classification of merchandise targeted at a specific customer base.

private label or **store brand** Merchandise that is developed exclusively for a retail store to its specifications.

quantity discount Discount extended to a buyer for ordering a large amount of merchandise.

quota A limit placed on the number of items that can be imported into the United States, by category, for each country.

receipt of goods (ROG) dating Dating as of receipt of goods; the date the merchandise is delivered to the store is used to determine the payment period.

regular dating Type of dating in which the cash discount and net periods are figured from the date of the invoice.

resource A manufacturer or vendor of merchandise.

returns to vendor (RTVs) Merchandise returned to the vendor because of damaged goods, incorrect shipments, or overstocks. Another term used is return to manufacturer (RTM).

rounders A type of display fixture that is round and is used to show apparel. It is usually found in the back of a department.

sales representative Person employed by a manufacturer or wholesaler to show a line of merchandise to store buyers and to take orders on merchandise selected.

seasonal discount (incentive purchasing) Discount offered on merchandise bought before the normal buying season.

senior assistant buyer See *associate buyer*.

six-month merchandise plan A plan that budgets dollars spent on merchandise in relation to projected sales.

sourcing Determining how and where a garment or item will be produced.

specification (spec) sheets Forms used to detail all specifications needed to produce a garment or item.

stock-to-sales ratio Inventory-planning method whereby the buyer establishes a relationship or ratio of stock (BOM) to sales on a monthly basis.

style out Method that checks for duplication or overlap used by buyers to review merchandise selected before writing the order.

subclassification A further division of a merchandise classification.

target customer A specific type of potential customer that either a manufacturer or a retailer is trying to reach through the development of new product.

terms of the sale Final agreement for sale, as a result of negotiation between the manufacturer or wholesaler and the retail store, concerning the transportation, delivery time frame, and amount of payment for merchandise purchased.

trade discount A percentage or percentages deducted from the retail list price of merchandise.

trade publications Newspapers, magazines, or newsletters published for a specific industry and available to professionals in the field.

trade show An exhibit of merchandise for a specific period of time, during which vendors show and sell their merchandise to retail store buyers.

t-stand A type of display fixture that has two sides and is often used to show merchandise coordinates.

turnover The rate or velocity at which the average stock has been sold and the money earned reinvested into merchandise within a given period.

unit sales reports A sales report provided to buyers that denotes what has sold by style or SKU (sales keeping unit) number.

variable expenses Costs that the buyer can manipulate or change.

vendor co-op Agreement by the vendor to share the expense of advertising or a special in-store event.

vendor matrix Spreadsheet showing a report of a vendor analysis including total sales, markdowns and gross margin.

waterfalls A type of display fixture that cascades merchandise and is often used to merchandise coordinating apparel.

weeks of supply The number of weeks it will take to sell the supply of inventory, calculated by dividing the current stock units or dollars by the unit or dollar sales per week.

World Trade Organization (WTO) An organization of many nations that controls trading practices, many of which involve apparel and textiles.

Bibliography

Burns, Leslie Davis, and Nancy O. Bryant. *The Business of Fashion*. 2nd ed. New York: Fairchild Books, 2002.

Carter, Linda. "How to be Profitable During Both Good and Bad Times - Open-to-buy." *The Retail Management Advisors*, www.the-retail-advisor.com (accessed February 4, 2014).

Carter, Linda. "The Retailer's Calendar." *The Retail Management Advisors*, www .the-retail-advisor.com (accessed February 4, 2014).

Carter, Linda. "What Is Stock Turn Rate and Just Why Is It So Important?" *The Retail Management Advisors*, www.the-retail-advisor.com (accessed February 4, 2014).

Clodfelter, Richard. *Making Buying Decisions: Using the Computer as a Tool*. 2nd ed. New York: Fairchild Books, 2002.

Connell, Dana D. *A Buyer's Life: A Concise Guide to Retail Planning and Forecasting*. New York: Fairchild Books, 2010.

_____. *Retail Buying: From Basics to Fashion*. 2nd ed. New York: Fairchild Books, 2002.

Danzinger, Pamela N. *Putting the Luxe Back in Luxury*. Ithaca, NY: Paramount Market Publishing, 2011.

Davis, Kevin. "Eight Sources of Power in a Sales Negotiation." WebProNews (April 2002), www.webpronews.com (accessed December 27, 2007).

Diamond, Jay, and Ellen Diamond. *Fashion Advertising and Promotion*, New York: Fairchild Books, 1996.

Diamond, Jay, and Gerald Pintel. *Retail Buying*. 9th ed. Upper Saddle River, NJ: Prentice Hall, 2013.

Directory of Major Malls, www.shoppingcenters.com (accessed November 2013).

Dlabay, Les, and James C. Scott. *Business in a Global Economy*. Cincinnati, OH: South-Western Educational Publishing, 1996.

Fiore, Ann Marie, and Patricia Anne Kimle. *Understanding Aesthetics for the Merchandising and Design Professional*. New York: Fairchild Books, 1997.

Gil, Liliana. "Five Reasons Why Upscale Latinos Represent the Next Market Boom." Fox News Latino (June 11, 2013), http://latino.foxnews.com/latino/opinion/2013 /06/11/five-reasons-why-upscale-latinos-represent-next-market-boom/

Guthrie, Karen M., and Rose J. Regni. *Perry's Department Store: A Product Development Simulation*. New York: Fairchild Books, 2006.

Jernigan, M. H., and C. R. Easterling. *Fashion Merchandising and Marketing*. New York: Macmillan, 1990.

Lamb, Michelle. *The Trend Curve, April 2014*. Marketing Directions, 2014.

Lamb, Michelle. *The Trend Curve, February 2014*. Marketing Directions, 2014.

Latz, Marty. "Cross-Cultural Negotiations Present Special Challenges." *The Business Journal of Phoenix* (December 10, 2004), www.bizjournals.com (accessed December 27, 2007).

LeBaron, Michelle. "Culture-Based Negotiation Styles." Beyond Intractability (July 2003), www.beyondintractability.org (accessed December 27, 2007).

Lindner, Steven. *Retail Accountability: Advanced Retail Profitability Analysis*. New York: Fairchild Books, 2004.

Liraz, Meir. "Retail Purchasing: Buying for Retail Stores." Bizmove, www.bizmove.com (accessed February 4, 2014).

Martec International, Inc. The OTB Report. Martec International, (2013), www .martec-international.com (accessed February 4, 2014).

Neiman Marcus, Inc. 10-K Annual Report 2012. United States Securities and Exhange Commission Edgar database (2012), www.sec.gov (accessed February 2, 2014).

Nordstrom. 2013 Form 10-K. Nordstrom.com (accessedMarch 17, 2014).

Off The Cuff. "Saks Goes Private Label" (October 2009), http://offthecuffdc.com /saks-goes-private-label (December 2013)

Payne, Neil. "Cross Cultural Negotiation." *The Sideroad*, www.sideroad.com (accessed December 27, 2007).

Ramsey, Dan, and Windhaus, Stephen. "Profit and Loss Basics." Netplaces – Business Plan, www.netplaces.com. (February 2014)

Reamy, Donna W., and Cynthia W. Steele. *Perry's Department Store: An Importing Simulation*. New York: Fairchild Books, 2006.

Rosenau, Jeremy A., and David L. Wilson. *Apparel Merchandising: The Line Starts Here*. New York: Fairchild Books, 2001.

Saks Incorporated. Form 10-K 2013. United States Securities and Exhange Commission Edgar database (2013), www.sec.gov (accessed February 2, 2014).

Solomon, Michael R., and Nancy J. Rabolt. *Consumer Behavior in Fashion*. Upper Saddle River, NJ: Prentice Hall, 2004, p. 206.

Tepper, Bette K., and Newton E. Godnick. *Mathematics for Retail Buying*. 7th ed. New York: Fairchild Books, 2013.

U.S. Census Bureau. American Community Survey (December 2013), www.census .gov (accessed December 2013).

Waters, Shari. "Open-to-Buy Planning; Controlling Your Inventory." About.com Retailing, www.retail.about.com (accessed February 4, 2014).

Index

Please note that *f* indicates figures and *t* indicates tables.

A

A stores, 9–10, 13*t*, 17, 42, 88

Accounts payable/receivable, 2

Achievement motivation, 18, 20

Achievers, 18, 19, 20, 21*t*

Advertising, 2, 95, 96, 104

Allocator, 2, 118, 119

Allowances, 95–98

AmericasMart, 70

Analyst, 118, 119

Apparel markets, 70

Assistant buyers, 2, 3*f*, 4, 15, 118, 119, 120, 121

Associate buyer, 121

Assortment plan

  by classification, percentage, and dollars, 65*f*

  classifications in, 53–56, 54*t*, 55*f*, 57*f*, 59

  by color, 62*f*

  by fabrication, 61*f*

  introduction to, 53

  juniors' department, 60*f*

  market trip and, 69

  other factors in, 59

  price lines in, 59–66, 66*f*

  by size, 63*f*

  subclassifications in, 53, 56–58, 58*f*

  tasks of, 53

  by vendor, 64*f*

Atlanta International Gift and Home Furnishings show, 78

Average stock, 42, 43, 44, 51

B

B stores, 9–10, 13*t*, 17, 88

Balanced stock, 41

Basic stock, 42, 43, 118

Beginning-of-the-month (BOM) stock, 41–42, 44, 45*f*, 69

Believers, 18, 19*f*, 20

Bloomingdale's, 119

Branding, 108, 116

Brands, 10, 22, 25, 27, 74, 108–109, 122

Bulk estimates, 83

Business analyst, 118–119

Business of Fashion, 26

Business publications, 25

Business Week, 26

Buyers

  assistant, 2, 3*f*, 4, 15, 118, 119, 120, 121

  associate, 121

  assortment plan and, 53, 54, 56, 59, 66

  buying plan and, 33, 35, 36, 41, 42, 44, 46, 47, 51, 52

  as career, 121

  current market and fashion trends and, 25, 26, 27

  market purchases and (*See* Market purchases)

  market trip for (*See* Market trip)

  most important goal of, 96

  negotiation for (*See* Negotiation)

  role in product development (*See* Product development)

  role of, 107

  senior, 121

  senior assistant, 121

Buying and merchandise flow calendar, 28, 28*f*, 88

Buying groups and services, 122

Buying office staff, 4

Buying organizations, 70

Buying plan

  BOM stock for, 41–42, 45*f*

  components of, 31

  introduction to, 31–36, 32*f*, 34*f*

  markdowns for, 46–48, 47*t*, 48*f*, 49

  most common, 31

  OTB for, 51–52

  planning sales for, 36–40, 37*f*, 38*f*, 40*f*, 49

  purchases for, 48*f*, 49–51

  purpose of, 31

  six-month dollar, 3

  turnover for, 42–44

C

C stores, 9–10, 13*t*, 17

CAD systems. *See* Computer-aided design (CAD) systems

Calendar

  buying and merchandise flow, 28, 28*f*, 88

  4-5-4, 33, 34*f*

  Julian, 33

  market, 68

  retail-accounting, 33

California Apparel News, 26

Cancellations, 98–99

Career opportunities in retail buying

  allocator as, 118, 119

  analyst as, 118, 119

  assistant buyer as, 120

  associate buyer as, 121

  business analyst as, 118–119

  buyer as, 121

  buying groups and services as, 122

  DDP as, 120

  DMM as, 121–122

  GMM as, 122

Career opportunities in retail
buying *(continued)*
Internet and, 122–123
introduction to, 117
merchandise allocator as,
118–119
merchandise analyst as,
118–119
merchandise assistant
as, 118
merchandise coordinator
as, 118
MPD as, 119–120
overview of, 117
planner as, 119
senior assistant buyer
as, 121
senior buyer as, 121
websites for, 123
Cash discounts, 86–87
CFTA-DR. *See* Dominion
Republic-Central
America Free
Trade Agreement
(CFTA-DR)
Chain Store Age, 26
Christmas merchandise,
94, 95
Classification reports, 69
Classifications, 53–56, 54*t*,
55*f*, 57*f*, 59, 69, 72,
77, 78
Closeouts, 95
Clusters, 13, 13*t*, 14*t*, 17, 88
Color, 31, 53, 59, 62*f*, 77, 81,
83, 107, 108
Color preferences, 22

Communication, with
department's sales
managers, GMMs, and
DMMs, 4
Competitive negotiation, 92
Computer-aided design
(CAD) systems, 115
Consumer-behavior
profiles, 18
Cooperative advertising
assistance, 4
Cooperative negotiation, 92
Cost of goods sold, 102, 104
Costing, 109
Costing sheets, 109–110, 112*f*
Cotton Inc.
Psychographics, 17
Cross-cultural negotiation,
99–100
Cultural differences, 22
Cultures, 99–100
Customer charge accounts, 2
Customers
primary motivation of, 18
redefine your (*See* Redefine
your customer)
resources of, 18

D
Daily News Record, 26
Damages, 96
Dating, 93, 94
DDP. *See* Director of
distribution and
planning (DDP)
Decision making, 72–73
Delivery dates, 72, 86

Delivery times, 115
Demographics and statistics,
5–9, 6*t*–7*t*, 8*t*–9*t*,
22, 107
Department sales managers,
2, 3*f*
Departmental goals, 4, 73
Departmental inventory, 4
Designer merchandise, 70
Designers, 25
Director of distribution and
planning (DDP), 120
Discounts, 86–87, 94,
95, 96
Divisional merchandise
managers (DMMs), 2,
3*f*, 73, 75, 77, 78, 119,
121–122
Dollars, 55*f*, 65*f*
Dominion Republic-
Central America Free
Trade Agreement
(CFTA-DR), 114
Doneger Group, 122
Drop paper, 73

E
Earnshaw's, 26, 77
Electronic data interchange
(EDI), 83
End-of-the-month (EOM)
stock, 41
EOM dating, 87
Excel, 118, 119, 120
Experiencers, 18, 19, 20, 21*t*
Extra dating, 87
Eye contact, 100

F
Fabric, 109, 110
Fabric preferences, 107
Fabrication, 53, 59, 61*f*, 72,
77, 81, 88, 109, 110,
114, 116
Fall I, 78
Fall II, 78
Fashion, 26
Fashion director, 2, 3*f*, 27, 78
Fashion office, 2, 27–28
Fashion office directive, 81
Fashion trends. *See* Market
and fashion trends
Federated Department
Stores, 119
Fibre to Fashion, 26
Finances, 2
Findings, 110
Fixed expenses, 104
FOB factory, 88, 94
FOB point, 87, 88
FOB store, 88
Forbes, 26
Forecasting, 35
Fortune, 26
4-5-4 calendar, 33, 34*f*
Fox News Latino, 22
Freight charges, 94

G
Galleries Lafayette, 70
GATT. *See* General
Agreement on Tariffs
and Trade (GATT)

General Agreement on Tariffs and Trade (GATT), 114

General merchandise managers (GMMs), 2, 3, 3f, 75, 77, 78, 122

GfK Mediamark Research & Intelligence, LLC, 18

Google, 122

Gross margin, 104

Gross sales, 102

Guaranteed sales, 96

H

Holiday goods, 78

Home fashion market, 94

Home Furnishings News (HFN), 26, 77

HSN, 119

Human rights issues, 114

I

Iconic styles, 108

Ideals motivation, 18, 20

Identifiable colors, 108

Incentive purchasing, 86

Income statement
    components of, 102, 104–106
    example of, 103f
    introduction to, 101
    profit or loss regarding, 101–102

Industry news, 25

InfoMat Fashion, 26

Innovators, 18, 19, 20, 21t

International markets, 74–75

Internet, 122–123

Internships, 118

Inventories, 10, 41, 42, 43, 44, 86, 118, 119

Inventory control, 2, 52

Inventory levels, 10, 51, 74, 120

Itinerary, 70, 78, 79f, 80f

Itinerary form, 78

J

Julian calendar, 33

Just-Style, 26

K

Kmart, 114

Kurt Salmon Associates, 122

L

Labeling, 110, 114–115

Labor costs, 110, 114

Landed duty paid (LDP) cost, 75

Latinos, 22

Le BonMarche, 70

Lead times, 115

Li and Fung Limited, 122

Lifestyle items, 72

Logos, 108

Lord & Taylor, 119

Luxury labels, 108

M

Macy's, 119

Macy's Merchandising Group, 122

MAGIC. *See* Men's Apparel Guild (MAGIC)

Makers, 18, 19f, 20

Manager of planning and distribution (MPD), 119–120

Manufacturers, 25

Marais district, 70

Markdowns, 4, 13, 35, 36, 41, 42, 46–49, 47t, 48f, 81, 88–90, 96–98, 106, 118, 121

Market, 67, 74

Market and fashion trends
    buying and merchandise flow calendar for, 28, 28f
    fashion office for, 27–28
    introduction to, 25–27

Market assessment, 72–73

Market calendars, 68

Market information, 107

Market itinerary, 70

Market purchases
    buying calendar for, 88
    delivery dates for, 86
    introduction to, 77
    open-to-buy for, 81, 82f
    preplanning for, 77–81
    terms of the sale for, 86–87
    transportation for, 87–88
    visiting resources for, 81, 83
    writing purchase orders for, 83–85

Market trip
    buyer's role in market on, 74
    cost of, 67–68
    decision making on, 72–73
    developing key resources on, 73–74
    discovering trends while in the market for, 71–72
    duration of, 78
    getting organized for, 71
    international markets on, 74–75
    introduction to, 67–68
    market assessment on, 72–73
    market itinerary on, 70
    pre-market planning for, 68
    reasons for, 77
    research business statistics for, 69
    scheduling, 78
    timing of, 68

Market websites, 68

Market-planning guide, 81

Markup, 51, 69, 81, 98

Markup percentage, 49

Men's Apparel Guild (MAGIC), 70, 78

Men's Collection, 108

Menswear, 78

Merchandise allocator, 118–119

Merchandise analyst, 118–119

Merchandise assistant, 118

Merchandise coordinator, 118
Merchandise exchange, 96
Merchandise flow calendar.
    See Buying and
    merchandise flow
    calendar
Merchandise information
    systems, 2
Merchandise plan.
    See Buying plan
Merchandise signage, 4
Merchandise to be
    promoted, 4
Monochronic culture, 99
Motivation, 17, 18, 19f, 20
MPD. See Manager
    of planning and
    distribution (MPD)
Mrket show, 78

N
NAFTA. See North
    American Free Trade
    Agreement (NAFTA)
National Retail Federation, 26
Negotiation
    of allowances, 95–98
    cancellations in, 98–99
    closing, 92–93
    competitive, 92
    cooperative, 92
    cross-cultural, 99–100
    of freight charges, 94
    introduction to, 89
    of payment terms, 93–94
    preparation for, 89–90
    of purchases, 93

relationship power in,
    90–91
Negotiation meeting, 91–92
Negotiation skills, 83
Neiman Marcus, 118
Net other income, 105–106
*New York Times Style
    Section*, 26
Nordstrom, 118
North American Free
    Trade Agreement
    (NAFTA), 114

O
Off the Cuff, 108
Off-price merchandise, 95
Open-to-buy dollars, 72
Open-to-buy (OTB), 51–52,
    81, 88
Open-to-buy (OTB)
    monthly report, 82f
Open-to-buy (OTB) report,
    69, 81
Open-to-buy (OTB)
    updates, 4
Operating expenses, 104
Order form, 83, 84f
Orders for approval, 4

P
Payment terms, 93–94
Percentage, 53, 55f, 65f
Perry's Department Store
    simulation
    beginning of, 15
    buying and merchandise
    flow calendar in, 88

buying plan in
    (*See* Buying plan)
classification, percentage,
    and dollars in, 65f
classifications in, 53, 55f,
    56, 57f, 65f
color in, 62f
consumer profile
    worksheet in, 24
costing sheet for, 112f
demographic information
    in, 5–9, 6t–7t, 8t–9t, 22
distribution centers in, 88
fabrication in, 61f
as fictitious, 4
income statement in, 103f
markdowns in, 47, 47t, 48f
market and fashion trends
    in, 27, 28, 28f
negotiation in, 93
poor-selling items in, 97
price line, units, and
    dollars in, 66f
product sheet for, 113f
purchase order form in,
    83, 84f, 85, 88
purchases in, 50f, 51
redefine your customer in,
    17, 19, 22, 23, 24f
retail organizational
    structure in, 2–3, 3f
role and responsibilities of
    buyer in, 3–4
sales in, 36, 37f, 38, 38f,
    39, 40f
six-month dollar plan in,
    31, 32f, 33, 35

size in, 63f
specification sheet for, 111f
statistical information in,
    9–14, 11t–12t, 13t, 14t
subclassifications in, 58f
turnover in, 42, 44, 45f
vendor in, 64f
Personal space, 100
Planned purchases, 69
Planner, 119
Planning/planned sales, 35,
    36–42, 37f, 38f, 44, 46,
    49, 52, 54
Polychronic cultures, 99
Pre-market planning, 68
Price, 81
Price lines, 53, 59, 66, 66f, 78
Price points, 51, 53, 70, 72,
    77, 106, 107
Price zones, 70
Primary motivation, 17, 18,
    19f, 20
Prints and patterns, 72
Private label, 107
Product development
    background for, 107–108
    branding for, 108
    introduction to, 107
    product planning for,
    108–113
    shipping for, 115
    sourcing for, 114–115
    summary of, 116
Product development
    efficiencies, 25
Product planning, 108–113
Product sheet, 113f

Production notes or
    instructions, 109
Profit or loss, 101–102
Promotional plans for
    department, 4
Psychographics, 107
Public relations, 2
Purchase orders, 83–85,
    84*f*, 88
Purchases, 48*f*, 49–51, 93

Q

Quality, 81, 110
Quantity discounts, 86
Quotas, 114

R

Ready-to-wear, 78
Receipt of goods (ROG)
    dating, 87
Redefine your customer
    cultural differences for, 22
    introduction to, 17
    VALS for, 17–22, 19*f*, 21*t*
Regular dating, 87
Relationship power, 90–91
Rent, 104
Research
    buying plan and, 35
    of current market and
        fashion trends (*See*
        Market and fashion
        trends)
    vendors, 85
Research business
    statistics, 69
Resource list, 71

Resources, 18, 25, 29*f*, 70,
    71, 73–74, 81, 83
Retail organizational
    structure, 2–3, 3*f*
Retail planners and
    allocators, 2
Retail-accounting
    calendar, 33
Retailers, 25
Return policies, 96
Returns, 102
Returns to vendor (RTVs),
    81, 92
ROG dating. *See* Receipt of
    goods (ROG) dating
Rounders, 72

S

Saks Fifth Avenue, 108,
    115, 119
Salability, 109, 114
Salaries, 104
Sales
    planning/planned, 35,
        36–42, 37*f*, 38*f*, 44, 46,
        49, 52, 54
Sales associates, 3*f*
Sales data, 4
Sales goals, 4
Sales personnel education, 4
Sales representative, 71
Salespeople, 2
SBI. *See* Strategic Business
    Insights (SBI)
Seasonal discounts, 86
Seasonal goods, 94
Seating arrangements, 100

Self-expression motivation,
    18, 20
Senior assistant buyer, 121
Senior buyer, 121
Shipping, 115
Shop the market.
    See Market trip
Shortage goals, 4
Simulation
    defined, 2
    introduction to, 1
    objectives of, 1–2
    Perry's Department Store
        (*See* Perry's Department
        Store simulation)
Six-month dollar buying
    plan, 3
Six-month dollar plan, 32*f*,
    59, 69, 77
Six-month merchandise plan,
    31, 35
Six-month plan, 33, 36, 44,
    46, 47, 49, 51, 52, 66,
    78, 81
Size, 26, 53, 59, 63*f*, 77,
    83, 110
Size ranges, 22
Social media, 2, 4
Sourcing, 109, 114–115
Special promotions, 4
Specification (spec) sheets,
    109–110, 111*f*
Speed-to-market, 25
Spring merchandise, 78
SRI International, 18
Statistical information, 9–14,
    11*t*–12*t*, 13*t*, 14*t*

Stock
    average, 42, 43, 44, 51
    balanced, 41
    basic, 42, 43, 118
    BOM, 41–42, 44, 45*f*, 69
    EOM, 41
    purchases and, 49
Stock assortment plan,
    77, 78
Stock assortment
    strategy, 77
Stock plans, 3, 4
Stock turnover, 51
Stock-to-sales ratio, 98
Stock-to-sales ratio method,
    41, 44
Store, 83
Store brand, 107
Store managers, 2, 3*f*
Stores Magazine, 26
Strategic Business Insights
    (SBI), 18
Strivers, 18, 19*f*, 20
Style, 31, 53, 69, 72, 81,
    83, 85, 88, 107,
    108, 109
Style number, 81, 110
Style out, 73
Style preferences, 22
Styling, 81
Subclassifications, 53, 56–58,
    58*f*, 77
Substitutions, 96
Summer apparel, 78
*Survey of the American
    Consumer, The*, 18
Survivors, 18, 19*f*, 20

T

Target Corporation, 118, 119
Target customer, 107
Target Sourcing Services/
    AMC, 122
Technology, 115
Terms of the sale, 86–87
Testing, 114
Thinkers, 18, 19, 20, 21*t*
Trade discounts, 86
Trade magazines, 77
Trade publications, 25, 26
Trade shows, 25
Transfer requests, 4
Transitional, 78
Transportation, 87–88
Travel itinerary, 79*f*, 80*f*
Trend analysis, 3, 25
Trends, 71–72, 77
Trim, 110
T-stands, 72
Turnover, 42–44

U

Unit sales reports, 69
United Parcel Service
    (UPS), 88
Units, 77, 95, 102

V

Values, atttitudes, and
    lifestyle survey (VALS),
    17–22, 19*f*, 21*t*
Variable expenses, 104
Vendor
    allocator and, 119
    analyst and, 119
    assistant buyer and, 120
    associate buyer and, 121
    assortment plan and,
        59, 64*f*
    buyer and, 121
    DMM and, 122
    market purchases and, 78,
        81, 83, 85, 86, 87
market trip and
    (*See* Market trip)
negotiation for
    (*See* Negotiation)
planner and, 119
planning purchases and, 49
senior assistant buyer
    and, 121
senior buyer and, 121
Vendor analysis, 4, 83
Vendor catalog, 85
Vendor co-op, 71
Vendor matrix, 74
Vendor performance, 83
Vendor performance
    report, 69
Vice president of finance,
    2, 3*f*
Vice president of human
    resources, 2, 3*f*
Vice president of
    merchandising, 2, 3*f*
Vice president of operations,
    2, 3*f*
Vice president of sales
    promotion, 2, 3, 3*f*
Visual merchandising, 2

W

Wall Street Journal, 26
Wal-Mart, 114
Warehouse managers,
    2, 3*f*
Waterfalls, 72
We Connect Fashion,
    68, 75
Websites, market, 68
Weeks of supply, 41
WGSN, 25
Women's Wear Daily (WWD),
    26, 77
Word, 118, 119, 120
World Trade Organization
    (WTO), 114